Testimonials

A Rookie's Guide to Pool Table Assembly is the only book available that completely explains all billiard table installation, including slate and cloth. The book is very good and needed by the industry.
–Steve Lankford, U.S. Billiards.

A Rookie's Guide to Pool Table Assembly is the most comprehensive source of information concerning billiard table assembly, including felting and slate leveling.
–Craig Connelly, Connelly Billiard Manufacturing, Inc.

Pool Table Maintenance and Repair (Assembly) is a truly comprehensive book on installing a pool table . . . Any billiard business should have at least one copy of this reference book nearby. It's thoroughly illustrated with top-notch drawings that make every technique crystal clear.
--Thomas C. Shaw, Pool & Billiard Magazine

Mose, thank you for the advice. We finished the table, and it looks and plays great! We could not have done it without your book. Your step-by-step instructions were accurate and provided the information that we needed for a successful assembly.
–Rick Gavazza

Pool Table Assembly is organized into sections. Each is a logical division intended to help readers quickly find their area of interest to assemble any pool table.

Pool Table Assembly expertly explains all aspects of pool table and felt installation and leveling.

Pool Table Assembly: finally, an all-encompassing book for anyone wanting to assemble their own pool table.

Pool Table Assembly details all aspects of pool table assemblies.

Pool Table Assembly is a handy, concise, and informative pool and billiard guidebook. It is expertly organized and chocked full of procedures, helpful hints, and pertinent illustrations.

BOOKS by Mose Duane

A Rookie's Guide to
    Pool Table Maintenance and Repair
    Buying or Selling a Pool Table
    Pool Table Assembly
    Playing Winning Pool

Novels
    JC's Last Chance
    Coyote Stands
    Something Substantial
    The Great Pool Table Heist of Arizona
        (Obama and the Dixie Chicks)
   Bigg Dick: Real Justise
   Pussy Willows: A Bigg Dick Novel

Available
    phx**billiards**.com
    amazon.com and Kindle
    barnes**and**noble.com and Nook
    Google Books
    Apple Books
    Kobo
    Etcetera

Detailed and Illustrated Instructions for Most Pool Tables

POOL TABLE ASSEMBLY

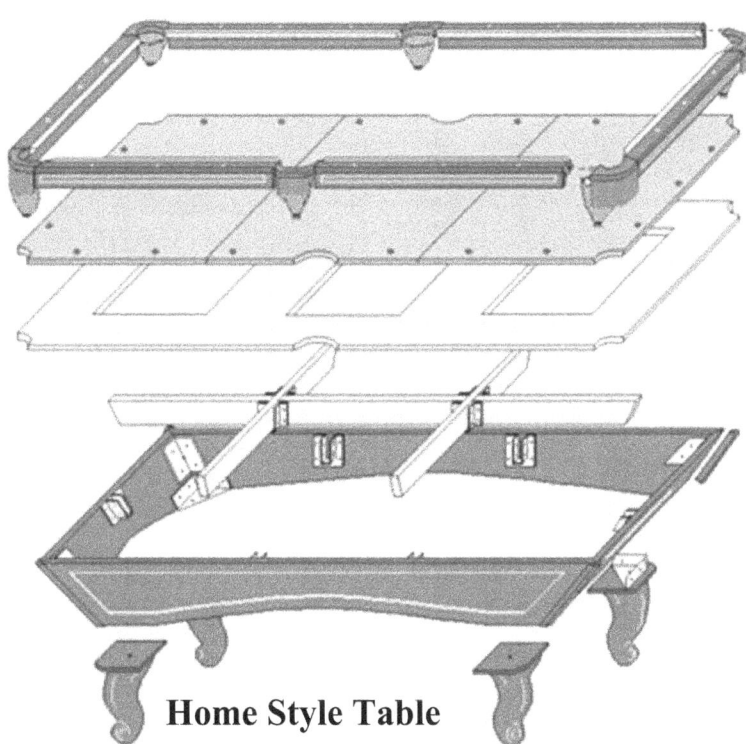

Home Style Table

Mose Duane

Copyright © 2004-2023 by Mose Duane

All rights reserved. This material—text and figures—is the sole property of the author and is protected under U.S. and foreign copyright laws. No part may be reproduced or redistributed in any manner or form without the express written consent of the author.

The purpose of this manual is to instruct and educate. It is designed to provide information in regard to the subject matter covered. It is sold with the understanding that the publisher and author are not engaged in rendering legal or professional services. If legal or other expert assistance is required, the services of a competent professional should be sought. Although the author and publisher have used care and diligence in the preparation and made every effort to ensure the accuracy and completeness of information contained in this manual, we assume no responsibility for errors, inaccuracies, omissions, or any inconsistency herein. All drawings and figures were drawn by eye, are for illustration purposes only, and are not necessarily to scale. Any slights to people, places, or organizations are unintentional. The author and publisher shall have neither liability nor responsibility to any person or entity with respect to any loss or damage caused, or alleged to be caused, directly or indirectly by the information contained in this manual. If you do not agree with the terms in this paragraph, please return this manual within thirty days of its purchase for a full refund.

Illustrated by the author

second edition

Publisher's Cataloging-in-Publication

Duane, Mose.
 Pool Table Assembly: detailed and illustrated instruction
for most pool tables / Mose Duane. -- 1st ed.

ISBN 978-0967808901 (first edition)

1. Pool (Games)   2. Billiards   I. Title.

What's Inside

INTRODUCTION	1
I TRANSPORTING	2
II MISCELLANEOUS MATERIALS	4

    Staples, Nails, Tacks, Seam fillers,
    Wedges, Shims, Tools

III POOL ROOM	7

    Distance from walls, Room dimension,
    Foot clearance, Floor and Ceilings

IV UNCRATING	11
V ASSEMBLY	14

    Cabinets, Legs, Slate platforms, Table positioning,
    Pre-leveling the cabinet, Installing the slate,
    Installing the rail cloth, Leveling the slate,
Filling the slate seams, Installing the bed cloth,
    Installing the rails and pockets, Fine-tune the levelness

Express Setup

If you are eager to get started, follow the balls.

(1) UNCRATING	12

ASSEMBLY

(2) CABINET	14
(3) LEGS	17
(4) SLATE PLATFORMS	18
(5) PRE-LEVELING THE CABINET	21
(6) INSTALLING THE SLATE	23
(7) INSTALLING THE RAIL CLOTH	25
(8) LEVELING THE SLATE	36
(9) FILLING THE SLATE SEAMS	43
(10) INSTALLING THE BED CLOTH	45
(11) INSTALLING THE RAILS AND POCKETS	58

Introduction

The need for this manual came about with the realization that far too many people are talked out of assembling their own pool table because we "professionals can do a better job." Nothing could be farther from the truth. Assembling a pool table is not hard, and with a little insight and this manual, any novice should be able to do a proficient job in an afternoon.

If you're a novice, read though the entire manual before starting your assembly so you'll understand each component and how it relates to others. This will make assembling quicker, less frustrating, and assure a professional-looking job.

If you already know enough about pool tables that you don't need the particulars, simply follow the express setup sections; each is highlighted and numbered by pool ball symbols.

Or, if you are mechanically inclined, just perusing my *most excellent* illustrations may be enough.

Also, there are many pool tables that have supporting frames instead of cabinets—the exposed portion of the table is not structural—and will assemble slightly different than those depicted here, but the only difference is in the frame assembly itself and interior pockets, maybe. The rest of the table —slate, rails, etc.—will be the same.

Enjoy.

Mose Duane

I / Transporting

Care must be taken when transporting any pool table, whether it is being moved from one room to another, across town, or traversing the country. If you have to pick up and deliver the table yourself, say from a trucking company's warehouse, it is probably advisable to leave it in the shipping packaging and crating (Figure 1-1).

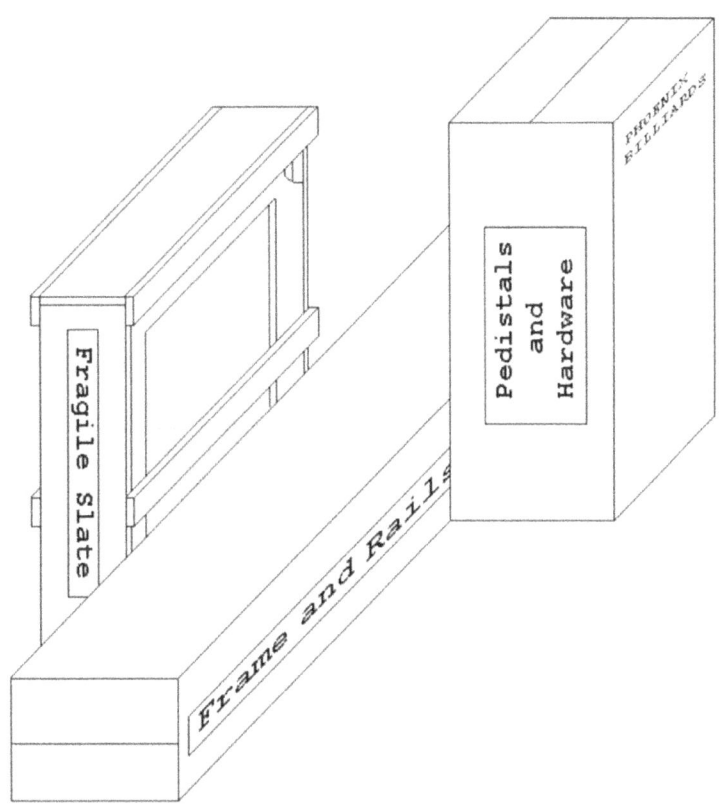

Figure 1-1 *Complete table in three packages.*

However, I have found it is lighter and easier to uncrate and transport in pieces, especially the frame (or cabinet panels) and of course, the slates, since they are usually packed all three in one crate.

If you choose to transport the table without packaging, special care must be taken to assure that the components, hardware, parts, and pieces are loaded safely and securely.

Slate can be individually hand carried, but, if possible, it should be wheeled standing on its edge on a mover's four-wheel dolly (Figure 1-2).

It is also commonly recommended that slate be trucked on its edge, tied securely to the front of the truck bed so it does not fall or shift. However, slate can be laid flat on the truck bed as long as it is not allowed to bounce or slide during transporting, which is how I usually do it. Make sure the truck bed is clean; do not allow anything to get between it and the slate. Padding beneath the slate is not necessary either. Any object that makes the slate lie uneven stands a chance of breaking it, however remote.

If laid flat, the three pieces of slates should be stacked, one on top of the other, and secured at the front of the truck bed. Nothing is needed between them. Padding on top, however, is a good idea to protect other table components.

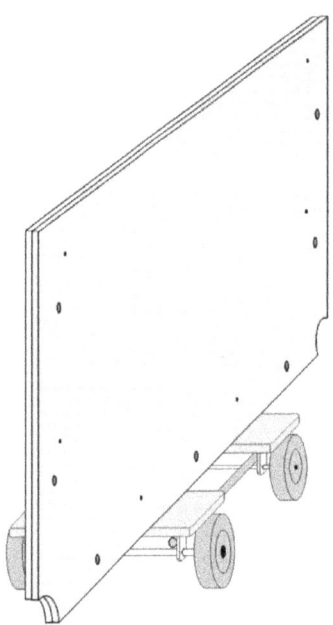

Figure 1-2 *Dolly good. Hernia bad.*

All cabinet panels, rails, and legs, if they were not packed in cardboard containers, should be wrapped in moving blankets, and can be laid on top of, and around, the secured slate.

A table that is to be stored for a long period before it is assembled should be carefully marked. All packages and hardware should be stored in a tight group and away from any work area where they could be damaged. Slate, whether crated or not, should be stored on its edge (not flat), and in a dry, shaded spot.

II / Miscellaneous Materials

Miscellaneous materials are the kind of paraphernalia you will need to assemble your pool table but are not pool table components. This is material that you usually will have to supply; they may not come with the table. These are all hardware store items.

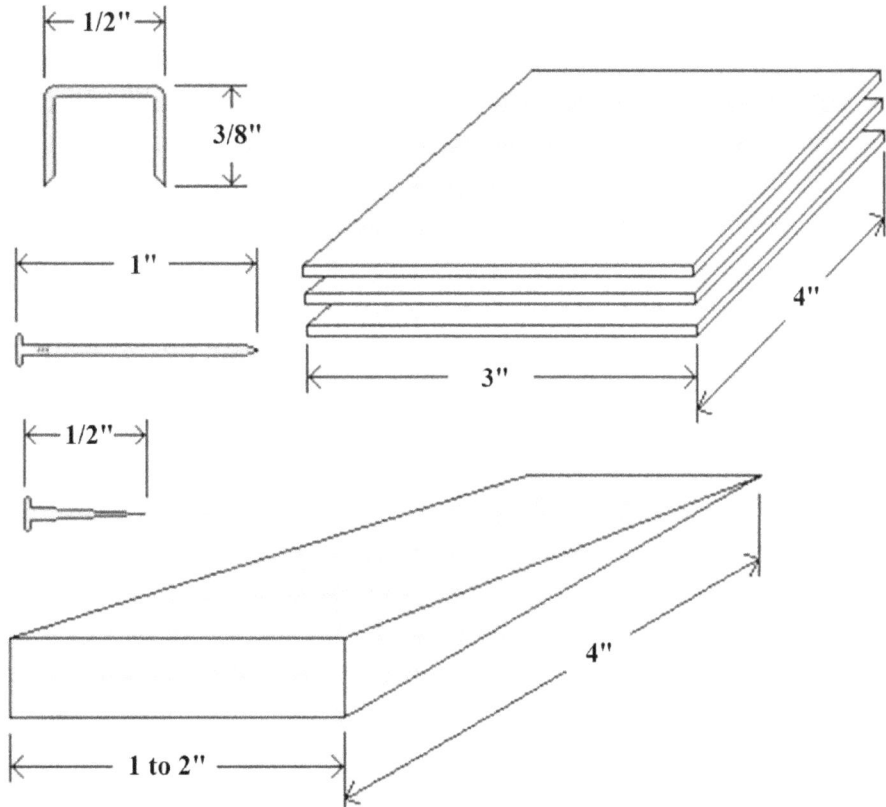

Figure 2-1 *Staples, nails, tacks, shim, wedges.*

POOL TABLE ASSEMBLY

STAPLES

For ease of use alone, staples are the preferred method of attaching billiard cloth to a table. Any commercially available hand or electric stapler will work. A pneumatic upholsterer's stapler is nice, but not necessary.

The staple's crown width is unimportant but is usually between 3/8 and 1/2 inches. The leg or penetration depth should be dictated by the job to be done. For billiard cloth, 3/8 inch should be used. Longer staples are not needed because they tend to bend or break instead of seat, so they will not hold the cloth anyway.

Staples used for leather pocket webbing at the bottom of the slate board should be either 3/8 or 1/2 inch long to penetrate the thick leather and still hold the weight of the balls. Anything longer is extremely difficult to remove, and, more often than not, will simply bend anyway.

NAILS

Small nails are required for the inside leather sheathing of the leather pockets. Pocket nails should be between 3/4 and 1 inch in length. Anything larger is unsightly, difficult to manage, and does unnecessary damage to the rails and slate board.

Three-quarter inch nails or wood screws can also be used on leather pocket webbing, instead of staples.

TACKS

Carpet tacks are sometimes used instead of staples to secure cloth to the bed and rails of a table. At one time, they were the norm, and rarely were staples used. Staples are faster, easier, and do a superior job, however. Large carpet tacks can also be used to attach leather pockets, but they are also unsightly when exposed.

SEAM FILLERS

Seam fillers are used to fill the countersunk screw holes and the seams in the slate. Three kinds of fillers are commonly used. The least popular but durable is auto body putty. Next is bees' wax, which is melted into the joint then smoothed over before it cools. And, because of its ease of use, the most popular is quick drying water putty, like Durham rock hard.

POOL TABLE ASSEMBLY

WEDGES

Wooden wedges are used chiefly to level the slate to the frame. Long, thin, and wide (1 to 2" x 4") wedges are superior to short, thick, and narrow ones.

SHIMS

Shims are flat squares of material—wood, floor tiles, sheet rubber, etc.—that are inserted beneath pool table legs to level the cabinet or frame.

GLUE

There are two types of glue used in pool table maintenance and assemblage. One is a spray adhesive used for bed cloth. 3M brand 77, 76, (or 90 in hot areas such as garages) are excellent examples. The second glue is contact cement, which is used for cushions, cue tips, laminates, and often bed cloth.

TOOLS

Staple gun (hand or electric), small hammer or tack hammer, Phillips screwdriver (electric power driver preferred), utility knife, putty knife, and ratchet and socket set.

III / Pool Room

Few homes are built with a pool table in mind; so finding a room of ideal size is rare. However, there are two ways to get around the size constrictions without poking holes in the drywall. One is a smaller table, and the other is a shorter cue.

Figure 3-1 *Arizona poolroom.*

POOL TABLE ASSEMBLY

DISTANCE FROM WALLS

Optimally, a room should be large enough to leave 5 feet of unobstructed clearance along each edge of the table (Figure 3-2). No wall, post, pillar, bar, table, or counter should obstruct a player or cue.

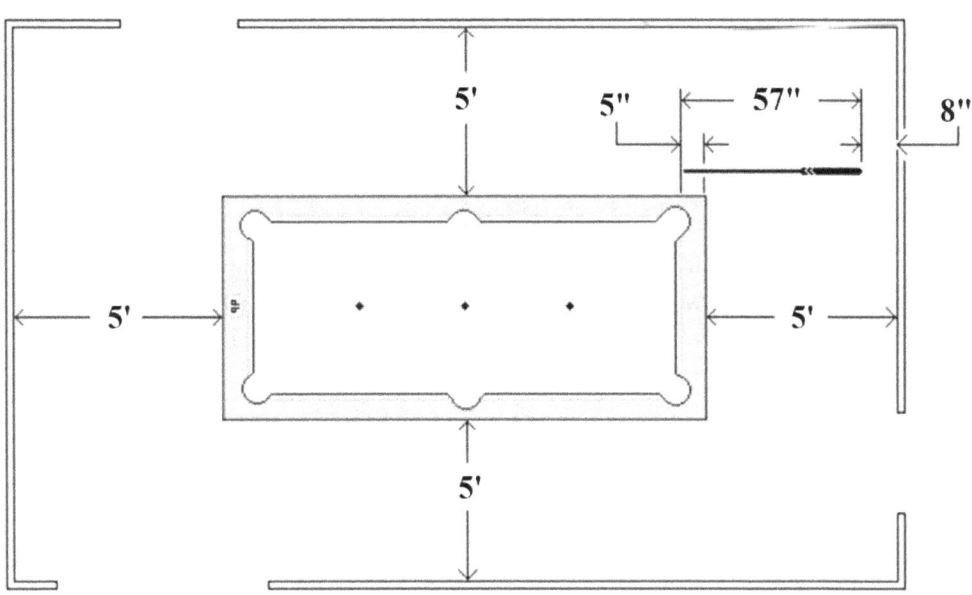

Figure 3-2 *Ideal table distance from a wall.*

Normally, however, most shots are at an angle to the rail with the cue ball away from the cushion. Because of that, the clearances can be cut by 6 inches and allow minimal, but satisfactory, playing conditions.

ROOM DIMENSION

Table 3-1 shows the optimum and minimum room dimensions for most pool table sizes.

POOL TABLE ASSEMBLY

STANDARD 57-INCH CUES

TABLE SIZE	OPTIMUM ROOM SIZE	MINIMUM ROOM SIZE
3' x 6'	13' x 16'	12' x 15'
3½' x 7'	13' 6" x 17'	12' 6" x 16'
4' x 8'	**13' 8" x 17' 8"**	**12' 8" x 16' 8"**
4' x 8' (oversize)	14' x 18'	13' x 17'
4½' x 9'	14' 6" x 19'	13' 6" x 18'
5' x 10'	15' x 20'	14' x 19'
6' x 12'	16' x 22'	15' x 21'

Table 3-1 *Room Dimensions.*

Room dimensions can also be cut substantially by using a shorter cue and figuring the distance from the wall as the same as the cue length. For example, using a 54-inch cue, instead of a standard 57-inch as in Table 3-1, a playable room size can successfully be decreased to 54 inches around the table; a 48-inch cue will decrease the room size to 48 inches around the table. A cue can be cut to any length. Shorter than 48 inches, however, the cue becomes too cumbersome for good control.

Table 3-2 shows the room dimensions for 54-, 52-, and 48-inch cues.

NONSTANDARD CUES

TABLE SIZE	54" CUE ROOM SIZE	52" CUE ROOM SIZE	48" CUE ROOM SIZE
3' x 6'	12' x 15'	11' 8" x 14' 8"	11' x 14'
3½' x 7'	12' 6" x 16'	12' 2" x 15' 8"	11' 6" x 15'
4' x 8'	**12' 8" x 16' 4"**	**12' 4" x 16'**	**11' 8" x 15' 4"**
4' x 8' (os)	13' x 17'	12' 8" x 16' 8"	12' x 16'
4½' x 9'	13' 6" x 18'	13' 2" x 17' 8"	12' 6" x 17'
5' x 10'	14' x 19'	13' 8" x 18' 9"	13' x 18'
6' x 12'	15' x 21'	14' 8" x 20' 8"	14' x 20'

Table 3-2 *Room Dimensions using cue lengths.*

POOL TABLE ASSEMBLY

FOOT CLEARANCE

The floor beneath and around the pool table also needs to be clear of obstacles such as ledges, steps, benches, chairs, boxes, camping gear, toys, Rottweiler, etc. This clearance should be a minimum of 4 feet from the outer edge of the pool table (Figure 3-3). If clearance is not provided, a proper cuing stance cannot be obtained. Tripping over, kicking, and stepping around floor obstructions and furniture detracts greatly from the playability of the table and concentration on the game. Also, using the area beneath the table for storage, however convenient, can be an obstruction, not to mention tacky.

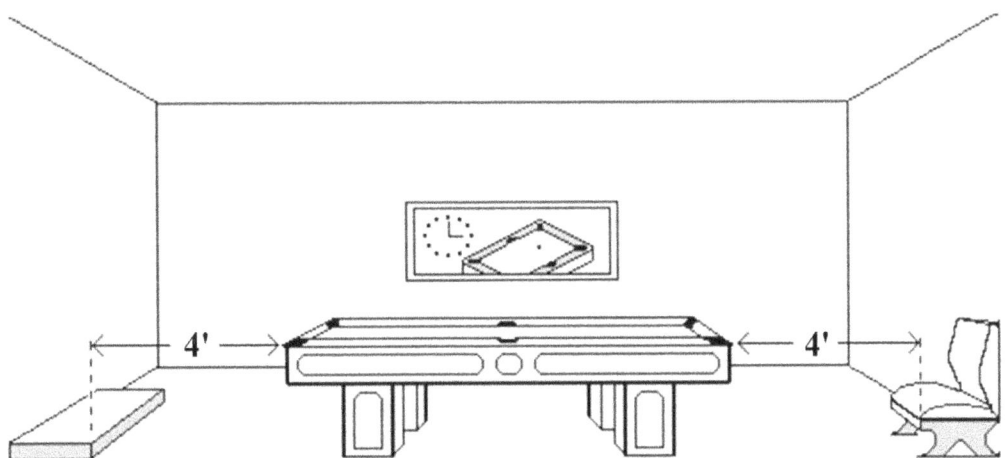

Figure 3-3 *Distance from obstacles.*

FLOORS AND CEILINGS

There is no recommended flooring material or ceiling height for a poolroom. A pool table can be leveled on any kind of floor—tile, wood, carpet—it does not matter, and carpet has the advantage of being quieter than other flooring

A throw rug under a pool table will also soften the noise of balls rolling when the table is on a tile floor.

Although there is no recommended ceiling height, it really should be over eight feet. Anything lower can actually get in the way of the cues and will get perforated by the cue tips.

IV / Uncrating

Often, tables will come in two crates or packages: cabinet/frame with all components—legs, rails, pockets, etc.—in one, and the slate in the other. Usually, though, each component will have its own crate or package making as many as six or seven, including the slate.

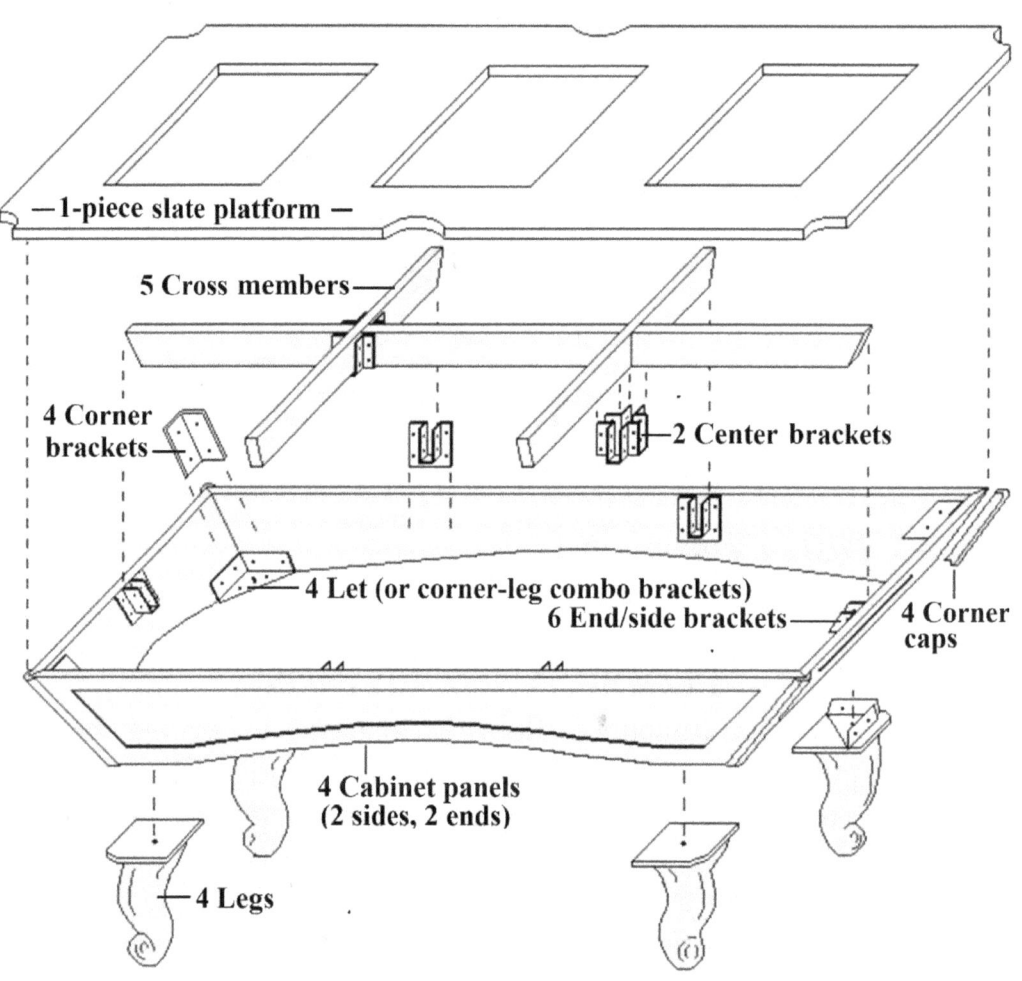

Figure 4-1 *Exploded cabinet.*

POOL TABLE ASSEMBLY

1 UNCRATING

Excluding the slate, carefully open each package and remove its contents. In parentheses, I have given the most common sizes. Although they may vary somewhat from model to model, their sizes will be close to those listed. An asterisk (*) indicates an item that may be substituted for another item.

In the hardware box there will be:
- 18 rail bolts and washers (5/16" x 2")
- 12 slate screws (1" to 3")
- 12 leg screws (1 1/2" construction screws)
- 4 leg nuts—or bolts—and washers (5/16", 3" bolts)
- 12 pocket bolts and washers (3/8" x 1")
- *A coil of rubber feather strips (1/4" x 1/4" x 16')

Lay all hardware out in individual groups according to size and type. These groups should be laid along a wall or some other location away from where the table is to be assembled.

If the cabinet needs to be assembled, you will need the following components (this list will differ slightly depending on table brand, model, and cabinet style you have, and sizes are approximate):
- 2 cabinet side panels (7' x 18")
- 2 cabinet end panels (3' x 18")
- 4 cabinet corner caps (2" x 18")
- 5 cross member beams (2" x 4")
- 6 end/side mounting brackets
- 2 center brackets
- 4 legs
- *4 corner brackets and 4 leg brackets, or
- 4 combined leg / corner mounting brackets
- 48 to 96 cabinet screws—or bolts (1/4" x 3/4")
- Slate platform (one-piece or 4 to 6 individual pieces)

Lay these on the floor in roughly their assembled position.

POOL TABLE ASSEMBLY

In the rail box there will be:
- 2 end rails
- 2 right side rails
- 2 left side rails
- *6 wooden or plastic feather strips.

Set the rail box aside for now.

The pocket box will contain:
- 6 leather pockets.
- *12 webbing screws.

Set the pocket box aside for now.

To remove the slate, lay the crate flat on the floor with the exterior slats up (Figure 4-2). Remove the exterior slats and remove each piece of slate. This can be done before the cabinet is assembled or after. I usually wait for the cabinet so I can take the slates directly to it. Although slates can be broken, it takes a pretty good jolt. So, handle them with care, but do not be nervous about moving them, either. And use a dolly (see Figure 1-2). Depending on the table brand and model, the slates may or may not have a slate backing board glued to them. The backing board is used to staple the bed cloth to the slate. If the slate is not backed, the cabinet slate platform will be used for the bed cloth, or the bed cloth will be glued onto the slate's edge.

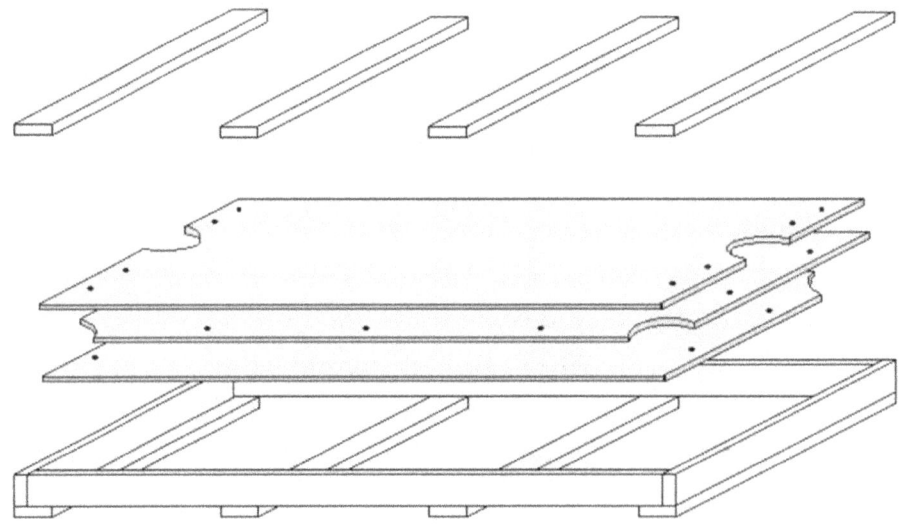

Figure 4-2 *Three pieces of unbacked slate.*

POOL TABLE ASSEMBLY

V / Assembly

Installation of a pool table, including covering the rails, is often time-consuming and frustrating, but it is not difficult and can be enjoyable and satisfying if approached from a knowledgeable position.

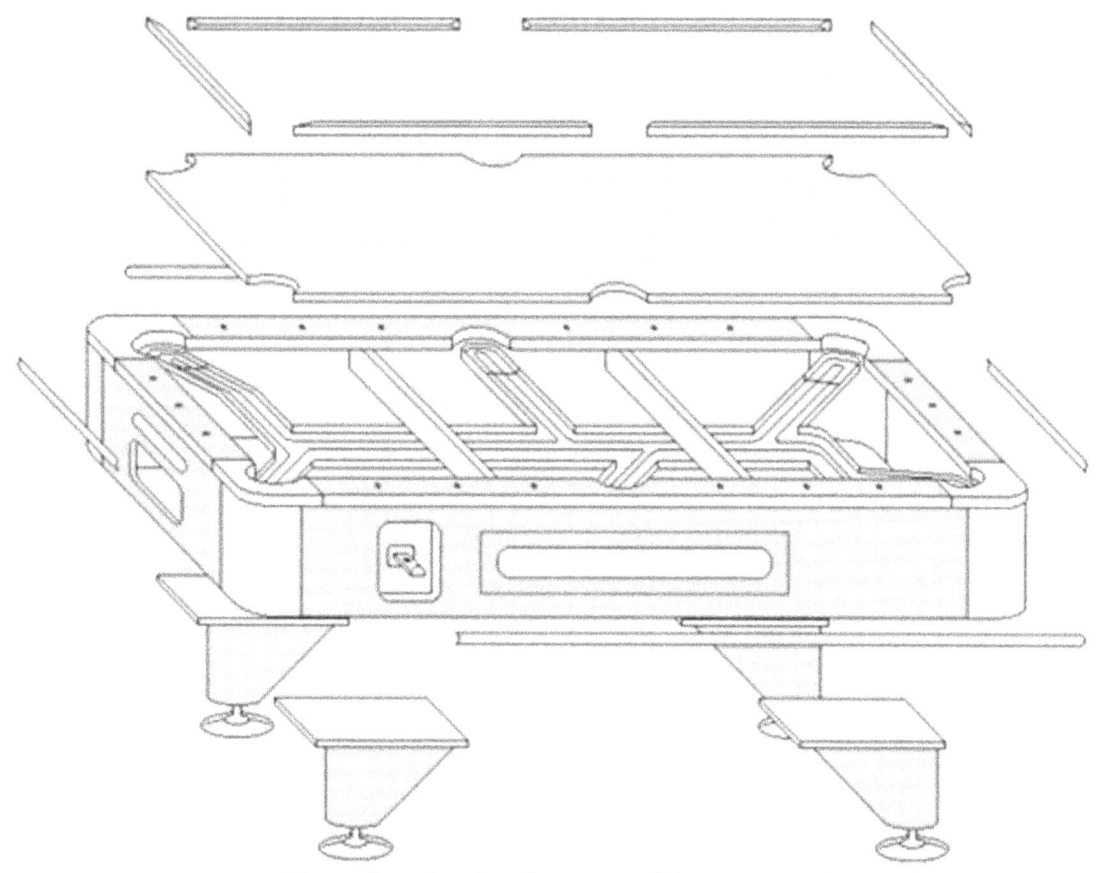

Exploded view of bar style table.

 CABINETS

All components and hardware—rails, cabinet panels, cross members, aprons, pockets, legs, screws, nuts, bolts, nails, etc.—will be packaged and labeled. Look them over to become familiar with them; visualizing the way they go together, and their function will make assembling much easier.

Occasionally the legs or pedestals themselves must be assembled before they can be attached to the cabinet. This is rare but, if so, assemble them first.

Pre-assembled cabinet

Some cabinets are pre-assembled while others are not. With pre-assembled cabinets, "assembly" simply means to attach the legs to the cabinet or frame; the rest of the table will already be together. If your cabinet or frame is pre-assembled skip to "Table Positioning" on page 19.

Unassembled Cabinet

Assemble the panels first, then add the cross members, the legs, and the slate platform last.

POOL TABLE ASSEMBLY

The cabinet panels are attached at each corner with wooden blocks (cabinet 1 in Figure 5-1), wooden braces with a gusset (cabinet 2 in Figure 5-1), metal corner and leg braces (cabinet 3 in Figure 5-1), or a metal corner and leg bracket combination (cabinet 4 in Figure 5-1).

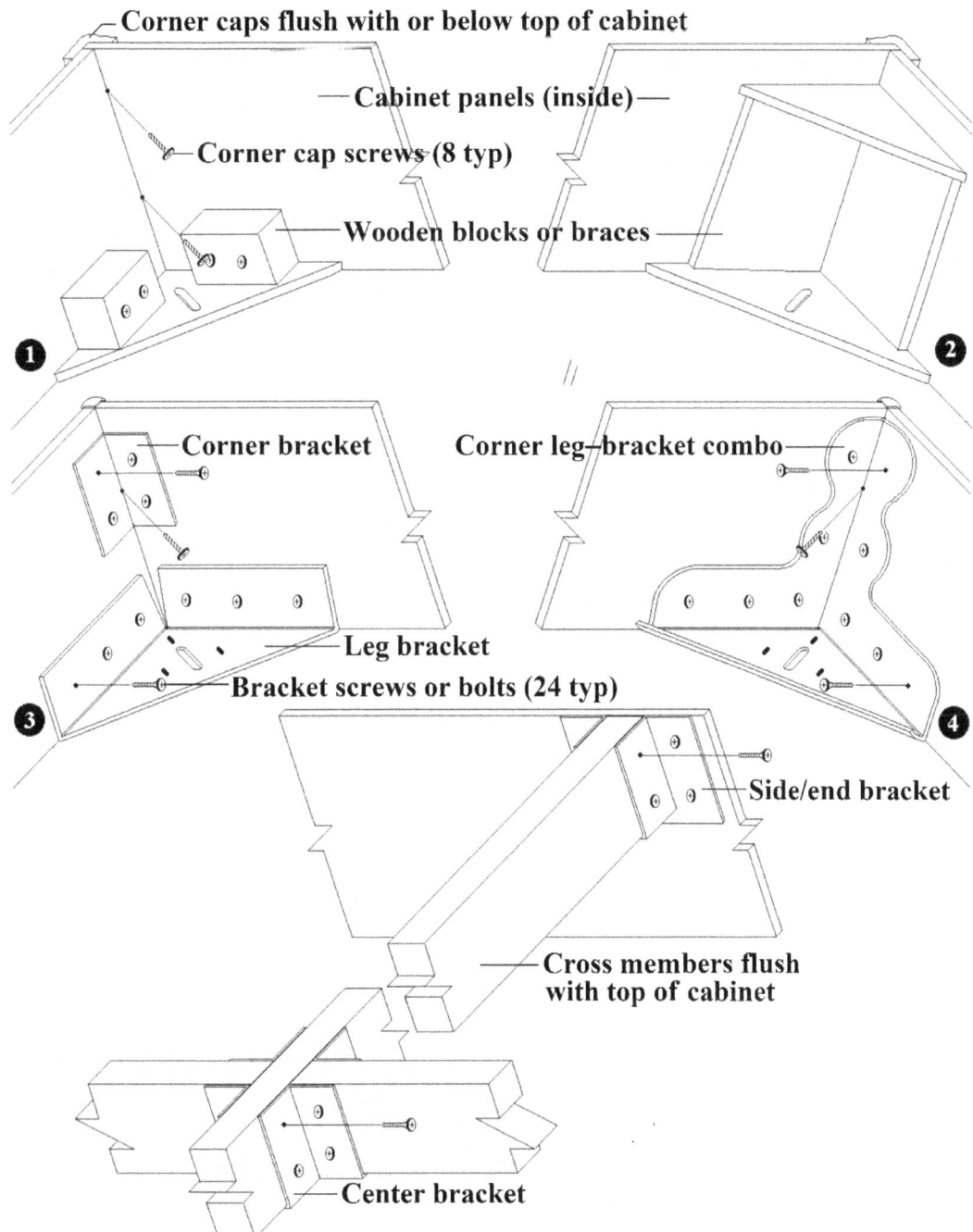

Figure 5-1 *Four different designs of brackets and braces.*

POOL TABLE ASSEMBLY

All cabinets will have some variation of the four corner-bracket or brace designs depicted in Figure 5-1. Whichever you have, make sure each part of the top of the cabinet (the part the slate or slate platform will rest on) is flush with each other (Figure 5-2). The corner caps should be flush or below the cabinet, but the bottom of the leg brackets *must* be flush with the cabinet's bottom. This is critical in the leveling procedure; if the cabinet or frame members are not flush there will be no easy or practical way to get the cabinet and slates level.

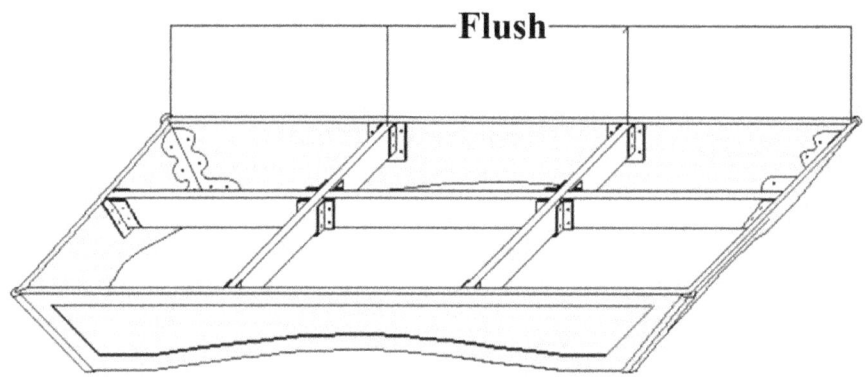

Figure 5-2 *Keep cabinet boards flush.*

Square the cabinet

To square the cabinet, measure it diagonally in both directions. These two measurements should be as equal as possible (plus or minus ½ inch) for the cabinet to be square (Figure 5-3).

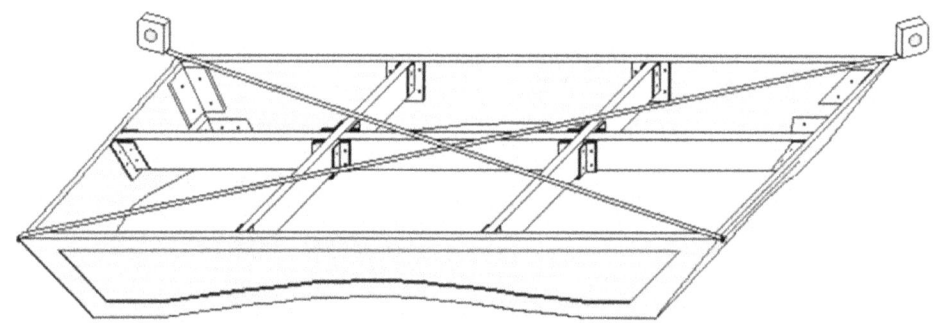

Figure 5-3 *Square cabinet.*

17

POOL TABLE ASSEMBLY

 LEGS

The legs depicted in most of this manual represent ram's head legs. Square, tapered, or other ornate or carved legs like Queen Anne, ball and claw, and so forth are attached the same.

Often, it is easier to turn the frame upside down to affix the legs, and then turn the whole assemblage right side up. With most, though, the frame must be set on the legs and fastened from above. Do whichever looks the easiest. Also, when the frame is turned right side up, do not allow any lateral force or weight onto the legs. If possible, rotate the frame in the air and set it down on all legs simultaneously.

As shown in Figure 5-1, some tables have separate leg supports and corner attachments and some are combined as a one-piece unit. These supports and attachments can be wood or metal brackets, depending on the table; however, the supports are usually assembled on the cabinet as it is put together so that only the legs need to be attached at this time, as shown on the cabinet in Figure 5-4. The exploded view in Figure 5-5 is provided for clarification only.

As you install the legs, visually check, and align each one; make sure it is not too far back, too far forward, or twisted left or right; the legs should look like they are part of the table, not some afterthought.

Tighten the center bolt or nut and then add the three leg screws to prevent the leg from twisting or turning.

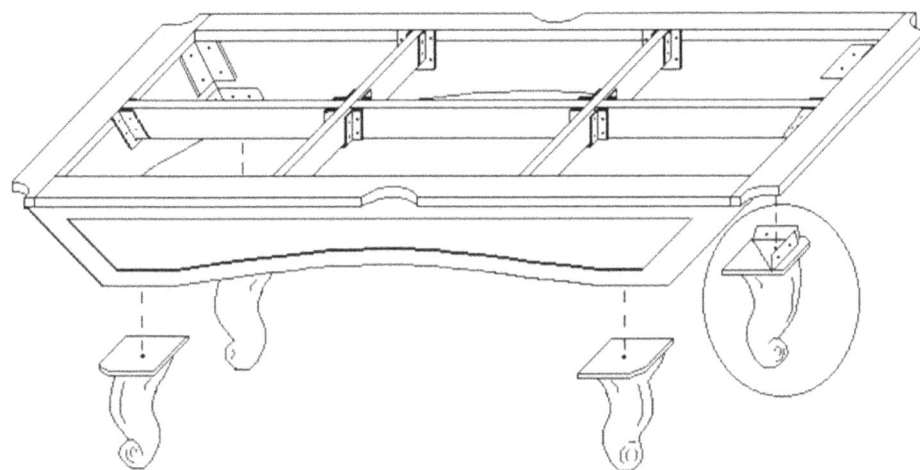

Figure 5-4 *Install legs to assembled cabinet.*

POOL TABLE ASSEMBLY

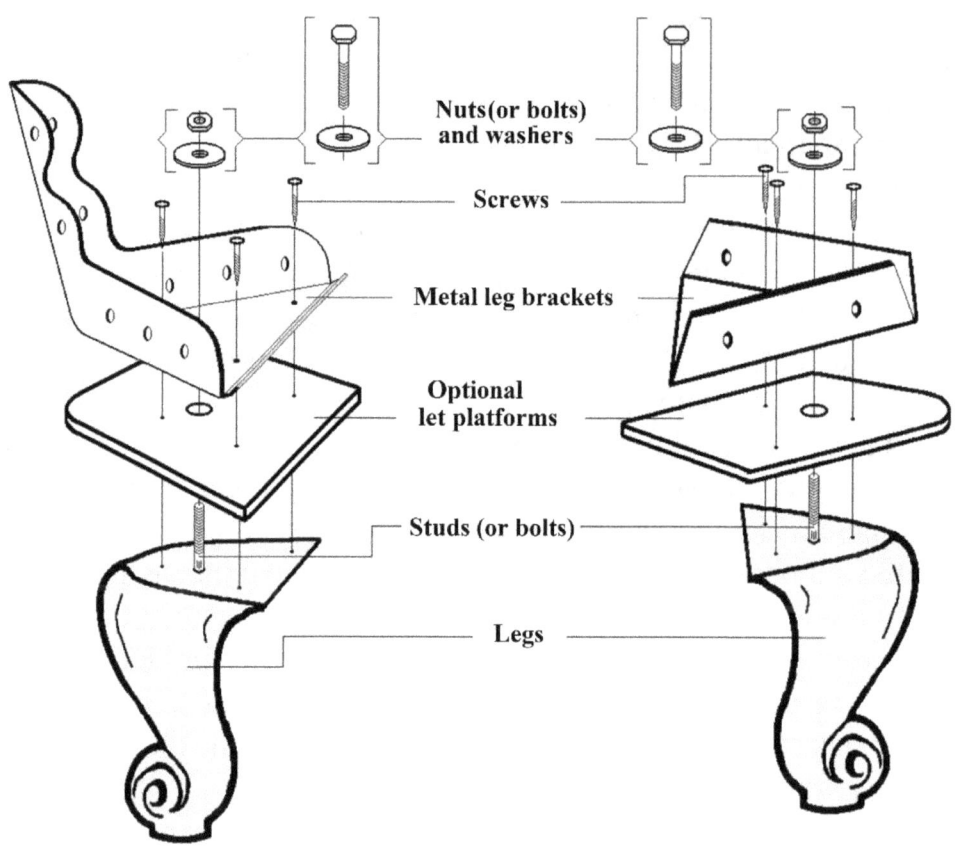

Figure 5-5 *Exploded vies of legs.*

POOL TABLE ASSEMBLY

SLATE PLATFORMS

On some tables with **backed** slate, the slate platform is narrow and does not extend to the width and length of the slate (Figure 5-6) and is used as a slate-mounting surface only. Also, on tables with **unbacked** slate where there is only a narrow slate platform, the cloth must be glued onto the slate (see page 51-57).

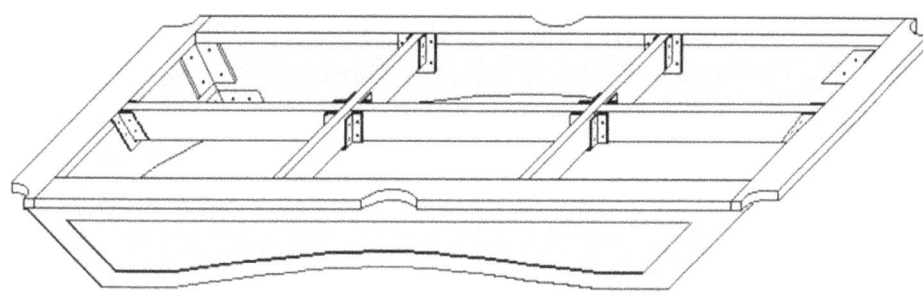

Figure 5-6 *Narrow slate platform.*

Other tables with **unbacked** slate use a wide slate platform for both a platform and something to staple the bed cloth to (Figure 5-7). These slate platforms are as wide and long as the slates. Depending on the brand and model, slate platforms can be one, four, six, or even eight pieces.

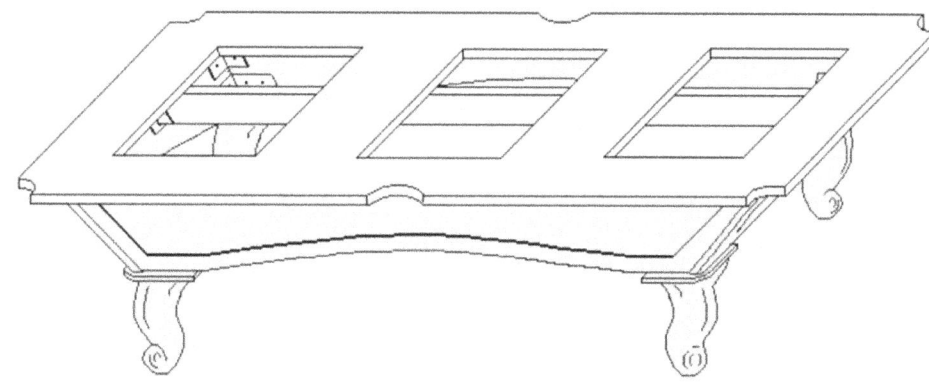

Figure 5-7 *Wide slate platform.*

POOL TABLE ASSEMBLY

The slate platform should be centered on the cabinet with an equal amount of overhang around the table.

Table Positioning

Once the cabinet and legs are assembled and squared, position the assemblage in the room where it is to stay. Determine which end of the table will be the foot and which will be the head. Often, they are marked, but if no markings exist, chances are, from the table's standpoint, it does not matter. From the room's standpoint, though, it does make a difference. The foot is the end where the balls will be racked when playing. That end should be placed away from windows, doors, mirrors, cupboards, and so forth. When a ball leaves the table, it is usually during the break, flying off the foot end of the table.

If the table is to be centered beneath a light, measure from two adjacent walls to the center of the light plate (where the light attaches to the ceiling), or, if the light is already in place, measure from the center of the fixture itself. Use those distances to set the centerline of the table (Figure 5-8). That should be intuitive and logical, of course. But you never know!

Or, if you have access to a laser light, simply center it on the table, pointing up toward the light plate or fixture. Then square the table with the wall. Use a carpenter's level placed across the frame as a base for the laser light.

Also, if the table is to be positioned in the middle of the room simply put the center of the cabinet in the center of the room, then square it with the longest wall—still intuitive and logical (Figure 5-8).

If, however, the table is to be offset to one side or end of the room, simply add 4 inches to the distance you want the table to be from the wall. For example, if you want your table to be the recommended 60 inches from a wall, simply set the edge of the cabinet at 64 inches. This can be done because the cabinet is approximately four inches (per each side and end) narrower than the completed table.

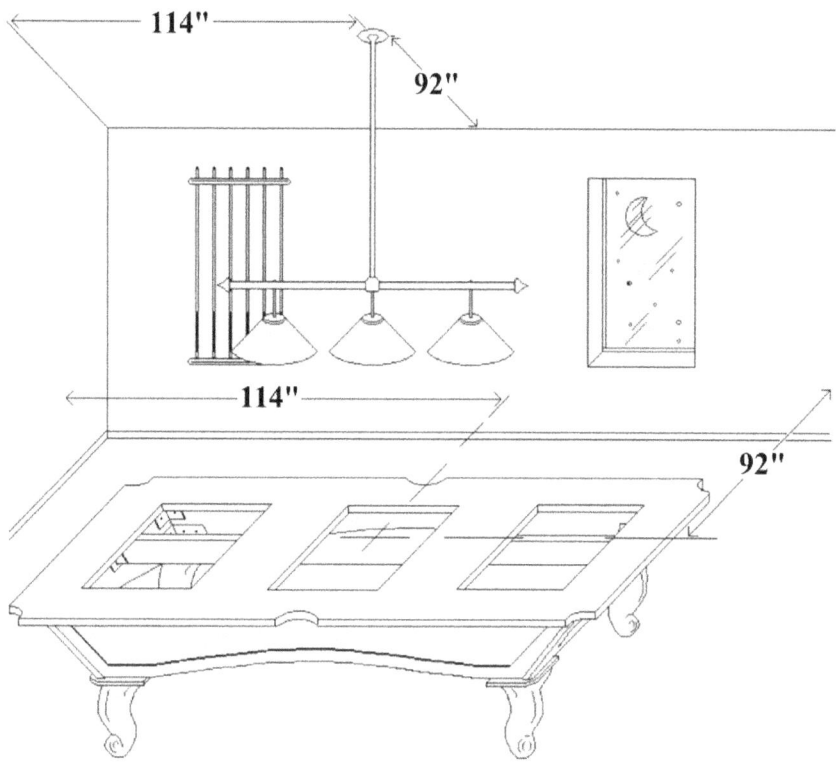

Figure 5-8 *Centerline distance under an existing light.*

Section 3 gives the proper distance the edge of a completed table should be from a wall, and once the table has been assembled it can be repositioned an inch or two to obtain these dimensions, if needed.

POOL TABLE ASSEMBLY

PRE-LEVELING THE CABINET

Once positioned, the cabinet should be leveled before adding the weight of the slate. To begin, check the cabinet from end-to-end to determine the high end (Figure 5-9).

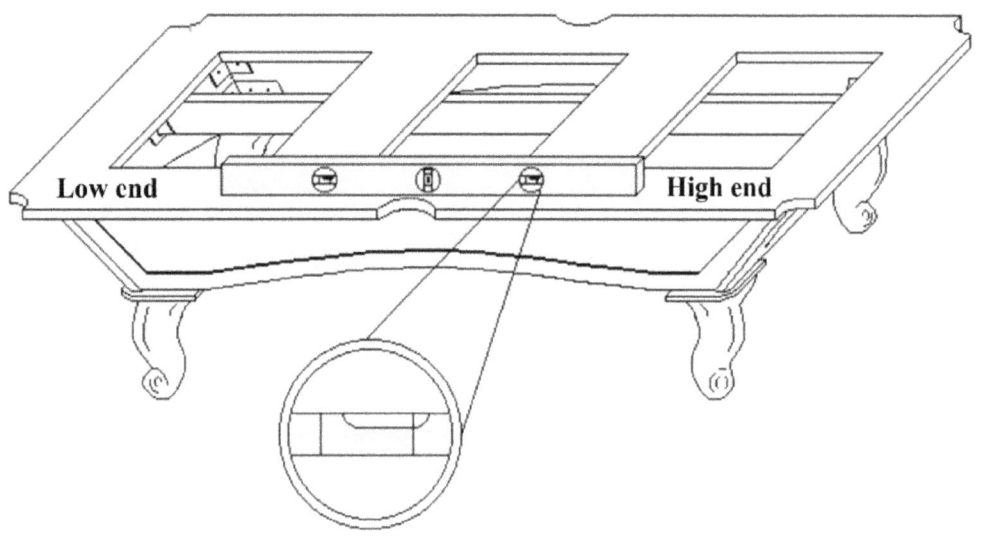

Figure 5-9 *Determine the high end.*

Use a standard 48-inch carpenter's level. If the cabinet is level, the bubble will be exactly between the two hash marks on the cylinder of the level. If one end is high, the bubble will be divided by the hash mark on the high end.

-Trick of the Trade-

Corrugated floor runner (available at most hardware stores) is ideal for leg shims. It is easy to cut to match the legs' footprints, does not compress, and is adjustable by placing the grooved faces together. Also, all four legs should not be shimmed. The leg that began as the HIGH LEG should remain on the floor.

The high end must be leveled side-to-side first. To do that, set the level across the high end of the cabinet (Figure 5-10).

POOL TABLE ASSEMBLY

The low leg must be shimmed. Shims can be any flat non-compressible material like wood, plywood, paneling, asphalt floor tile, or pasteboard, and should vary in thickness between 1/16 and 1/4 inches. Each shim should be cut to the size of the table leg's footprint, or slightly smaller, but for appearance, it should not be larger than that part of the leg that rests on the floor.

Add shims until the low side is level with the high side (Figure 5-10).

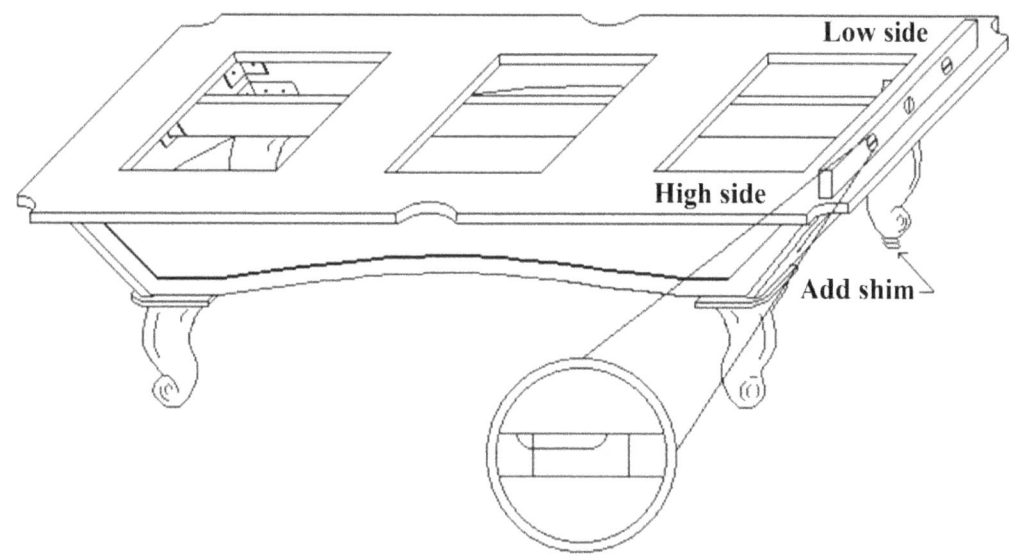

Figure 5-10 *Shim the low leg of the high end first.*

After leveling the high end, level one side of the cabinet from end-to-end (Figure 5-11).

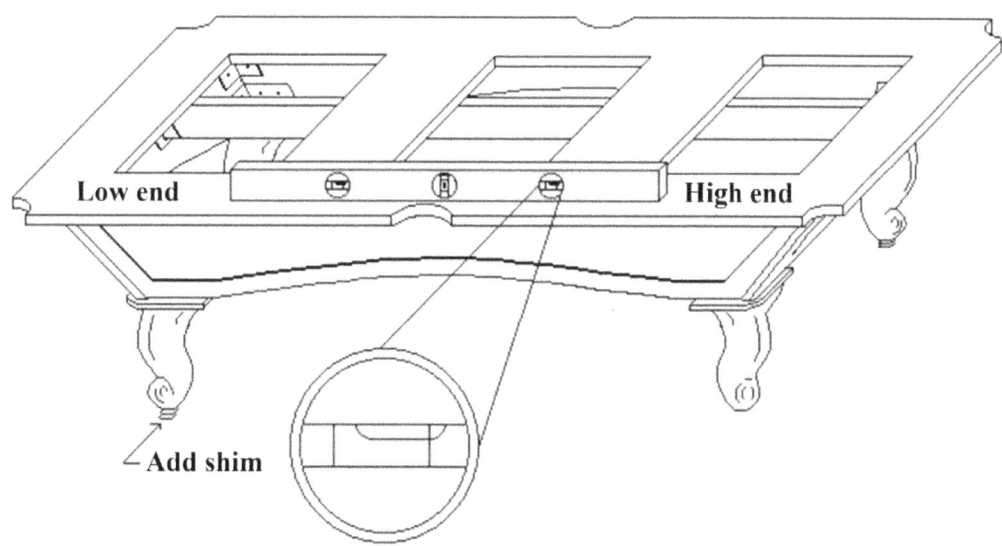

Figure 5-11 *Level the cabinet end to end.*

POOL TABLE ASSEMBLY

Next, level across the low end of the cabinet (Figure 5-12), when this is done, double-check the entire cabinet. Sometimes leveling one end throws the other end off.

Continue until the cabinet is level, or as near level as possible. Often, if the cabinet is not perfectly flat, it is necessary to split the difference between one side or end and the other.

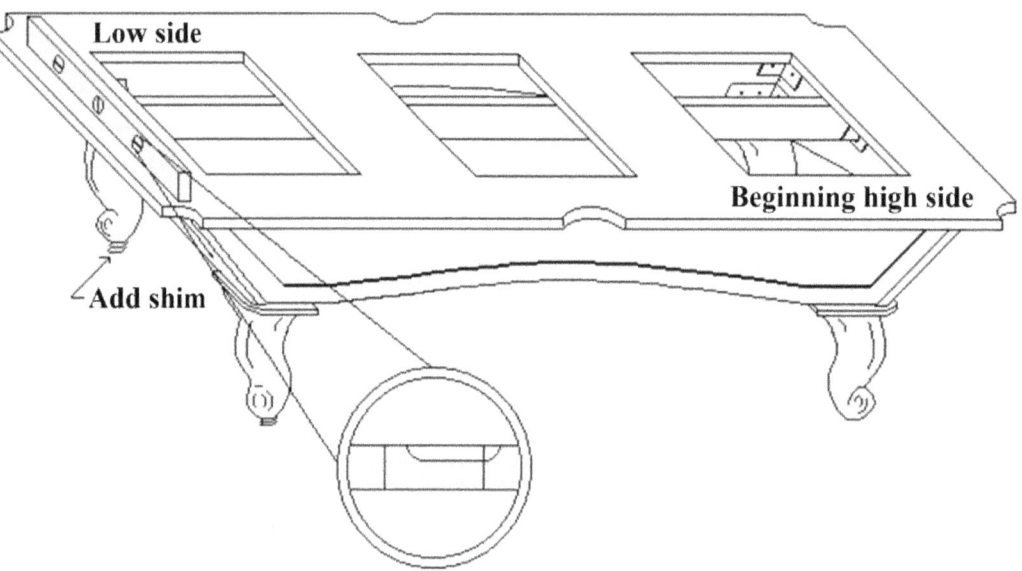

Figure 5-12 *Level the cabinet across the low end.*

 INSTALLING THE SLATE

It is important that the cabinet is pre-leveled and squared, and that all top members are flush with each other before the slate is set on the table.

All slates have a top and bottom, which should not be reversed. There are four ways to determine top from bottom:

1. Each slate will be marked, or have a slate board affixed to the bottom.
2. The top will likely have shallow circular grooves cut by the surface grinding process; the underside will be smoother looking, but it will not necessarily be flat.
3. Each pocket cutout of the topside should have a large and smooth radius curving into the pocket.
4. Slates screwed to the cabinet will have countersunk screw holes on the topside.

To install the three-piece slate set, determine first which slate goes at the head and which at the foot end of the table. Some slates are marked at the head and foot, but most are not, so it doesn't matter which end piece goes to the head or foot.

However, most three-piece slates are matched and precision ground as a set, so must be assembled in their matched order. The slates will be marked or numbered either on the face or by dimples at the edge of each piece where the seams butt together.

Again, slates that are not marked are not normally matched sets and, therefore, the end pieces can be interchanged without problems.

Position all three slates on the table. Slates doweled and pinned might have to be raised at one end or the other to align and set the pins. Measure around the periphery to ensure that each slate overhangs the cabinet or slate board equally on both sides and both ends. This also squares the slate to the cabinet (Figure 5-13).

POOL TABLE ASSEMBLY

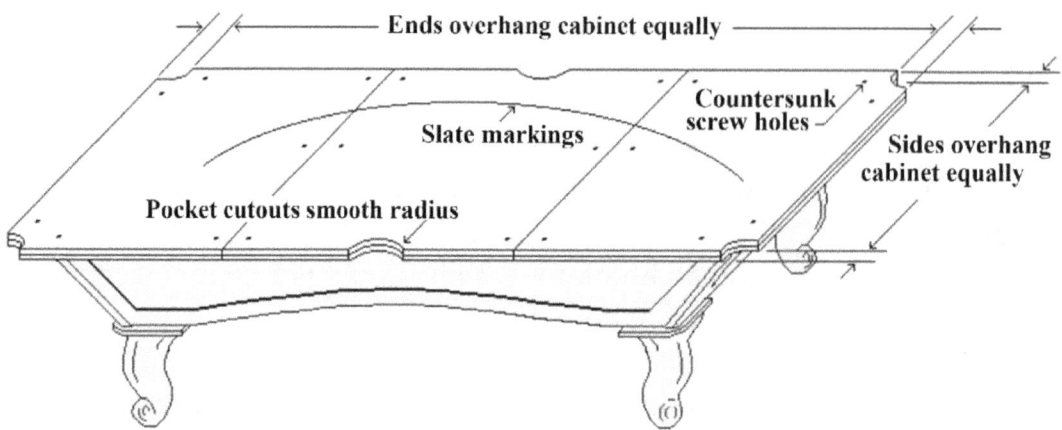

Figure 5-13 *Slate top.*

Wood screws are used to secure most slates, and pilot holes should be drilled into the cabinet or slate board to ensure that the slate screws go in without stripping the heads or stripping or splitting the cabinet or slate board.

Assuming 1/4-inch diameter slate screws, drill 1/8-to-3/16-inch pilot holes (the denser the material the larger the pilot hole).

Insert and tighten all slate screws to pull the slates to the cabinet or slate board snugly. This is important and must be done to ensure a solid starting point before beginning the slate leveling process (Figure 5-14).

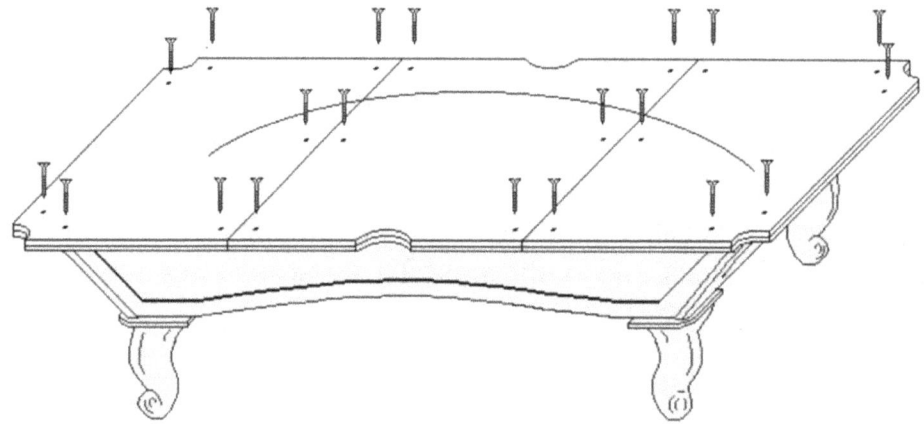

Figure 5-14 *Slate screws.*

Later, the screw heads will be filled with seam filler to get a smooth playing surface (see "Filling Slate Seams" on page 43).

-Trick of the Trade-
A small amount of dry bar soap on the wood screw threads will help them turn smoothly and easily.

If the rails on your table are already covered, lucky you; skip ahead to "Leveling the Slate" on page 36.

If, however, the rails need to be covered and you have to use the pool table as a workbench, cover them at this time.

POOL TABLE ASSEMBLY

⑦ INSTALLING THE RAIL CLOTH

An ideal workbench, with vises, clamps, and handy tool racks is nice, but it is not always easy to produce, nor is it particularly necessary. Although not ideal, there is nothing wrong with using the pool table bed as a workspace if you do it before the bed cloth is attached.

Simply spread a drop cloth across the top of the table to protect rails from scratches and dings, arrange all needed tools within easy reach, and go to work. Be aware, however, if you have already leveled the table some re-leveling should be done once you are finished with the rails.

Most people, including some pool table mechanics, consider installing the rail cloth to be more difficult than installing the bed cloth, but this is not necessarily the case. The following instructions are straightforward and easy to understand and, if followed, anyone can do a professional-looking job.

Some manufacturers ship the rail cloth already separated from the bed cloth, others do not. The following cloth-cutting guide has been provided if the rail cloth has to be separated.

Cloth Cutting Guide

Figure 5-15 shows how to cut the rail cloth pieces from standard width cloth for the most common size pool tables. Ideally, rail cloth pieces should be 6 inches wide and at least 4 inches longer than the length of the rails. Pieces 5 ½ inches wide can be used without problems and should be considered for 62-inch wide and narrower cloth.

For standard 62-inch cloth, cut four 54" x 6" rail cloth pieces from the side and two 51" x 6" pieces from the end (Figure 5-15).

If the cloth face is not obvious, it is rolled or folded with the face inside. Mark the edge of the face—or the back—of each piece, including the bed cloth. A pencil works fine.

POOL TABLE ASSEMBLY

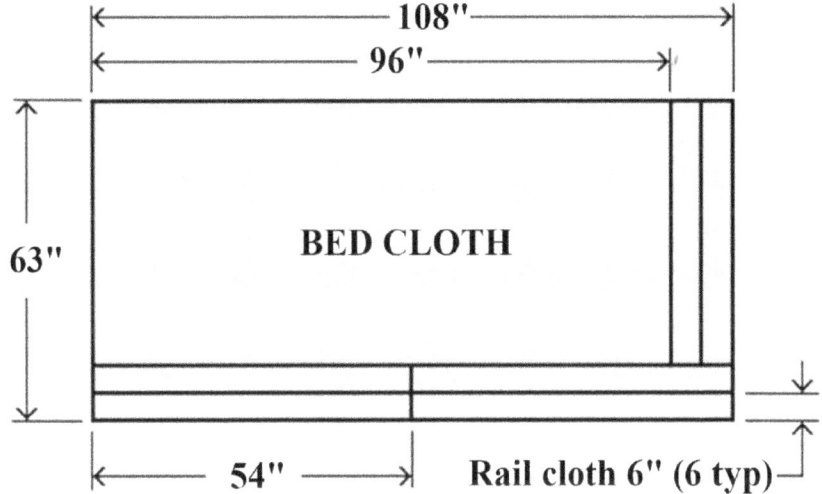

Figure 5-15 *Cloth-cutting guide for 4 x 8 tables (44x88).*

With 8-foot oversize and 9-foot tables, four rail-cloth pieces are taken from the end of the cloth and two from the side of standard 62-inch cloth. And all six rail-cloth pieces come from the side of wider 78-inch cloth, no matter what size the table is.

Feather Strips

Often, wooden feather strips are shipped already cut to size, but others need to be cut to their proper length. Laying them in their respective rail groove and mark the facing angle on each end then cut them at that angle, a utility knife or small hacksaw works fine (Figure 5-16). Plastic feather strips often come in one long coil. Using a utility knife cut the coil into six equal strips; each strip should be longer than the rails.

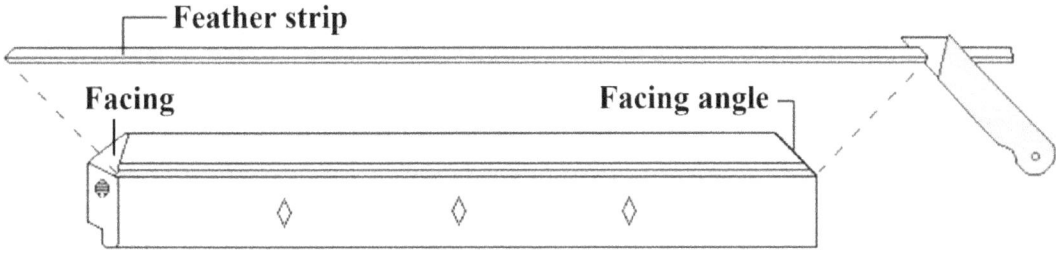

Figure 5-16 *Cut the feather strips to fit.*

A double cloth thickness clearance should be left between the facings and the end of the feather strip. Feather strips cut too long will bulge into the pocket opening, and those cut too short may allow the cloth to wrinkle at the top rail. Tighten loose (thin) feather strips by wrapping them with masking tape or doubling the rail cloth. Allow approximately one-half cloth thickness for clearance on each side of the groove (one thickness overall), and one-half cloth thickness at the bottom (Figure 5-17).

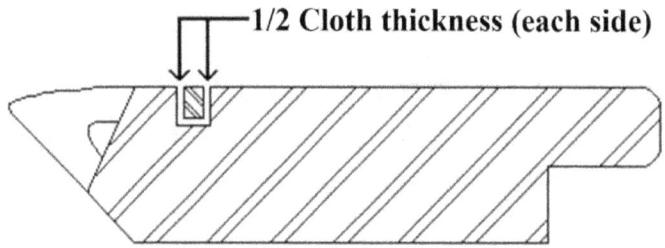

Figure 5-17 *Normal feather strip clearance.*

Feather strips that are too tight (thick) can be sized by simply eliminating the front space, allowing only one-half cloth thickness at the back. This works fine as long as the feather strip fits snuggly (Figure 5-18).

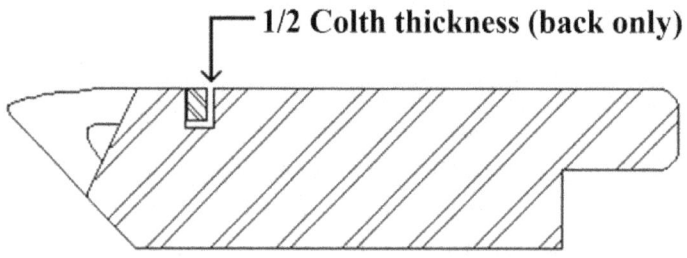

Figure 5-18 *Tight feather strip clearance.*

After the feather strips have been prepared, insert and center each into its prospective groove. Draw a line across the center of the feather strip and rail, toward the cushion, to show its relative position (Figure 5-19).

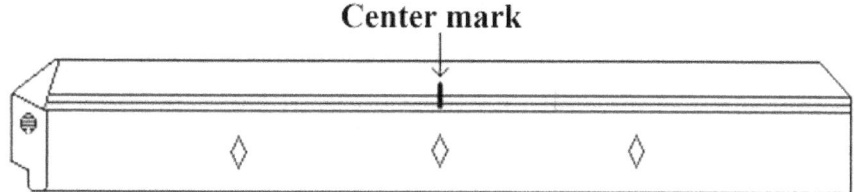

Figure 5-19 *Center mark feather strip.*

This mark will ensure that the feather strip can be returned to its centered location during the covering process.

The order in which rails are covered is unimportant, but it is generally easier to start with the end rails.

End rails and side rails differ in the way the pocket facing angles are cut. End rails have two corner pocket angles and side rails have one corner pocket angle and one center pocket angle. The angle of the corner pocket is cut wider than the angle of the center pocket (Figure 5-20).

These angles are treated differently in the covering process. The cloth is pulled over the facing of the corner pocket angle and folded over the facing of the center pocket angle.

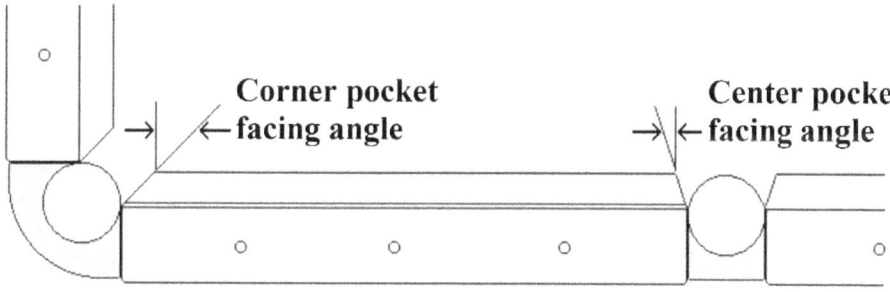

Figure 5-20 *Pocket facing angles, right side rail.*

POOL TABLE ASSEMBLY

End Rails

Lay the rail cloth *face down* on top of an end rail and, depending on how tight the feather strip is, extend one long edge of the rail cloth zero to 1/2 inch over the feather strip groove, and allow both ends to overhang the rail two or more inches.

Place the feather strip above the cloth and the groove and align the center marks (rail 1 in Figure 5-21).

Gently drive the *center* of the feather strip a quarter to halfway into the groove with a rubber mallet (rail 2 in Figure 5-21).

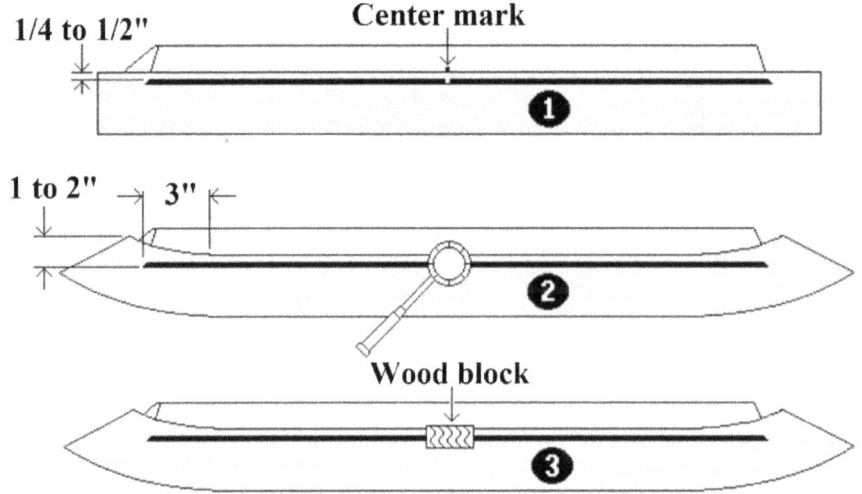

Figure 5-21 *Seating feather strip on end rail.*

Now, stretch one end of the cloth toward its end of the rail, maintaining the extension over the groove you started with. If you started with a 1/2-inch extension, maintain it; if you started with no extension, maintain zero extension. In other words, keep the cloth straight.

While stretching the cloth and maintaining the extension, using a rubber mallet, drive the feather strip a quarter to halfway into the groove. (If the feather strip is flexible plastic, stretch it along with the cloth.) Continue this until approximately 3 inches from the end.

If you are using plastic feather strips, they will stretch past the ends of the rails. Mark the facing angles and cut them again before continuing. Wooden feather strips will not stretch.

POOL TABLE ASSEMBLY

From that 3-inch point, pull 1 to 2 inches of cloth from beneath the feather strip, toward the cushion, making a triangular shape of approximately 3 x 1 1/2 inches (rail 2 in Figure 5-21). Keep the cloth taut and drive in the remaining section of feather strip a quarter to halfway into the groove.

Repeat the above process for the other end of the *end* rail.

Then, using a block of wood and a rubber mallet, drive the feather strip until tight or flush with the top rail (rail 3 in Figure 5-21). Keep the wood block flat and level so it does not damage the top rail.

Side Rails
Side rails are treated slightly differently because of the center pocket-facing angle. After completing the corner pocket-facing angle, pull the cloth straight toward the center pocket angle (rail 2 in Figure 5-22).

Using a block of wood and a rubber mallet, drive the feather strip until it is flush with the top rail (rail 3 in Figure 5-22). Keep the wood block flat and level so it does not damage the top rail.

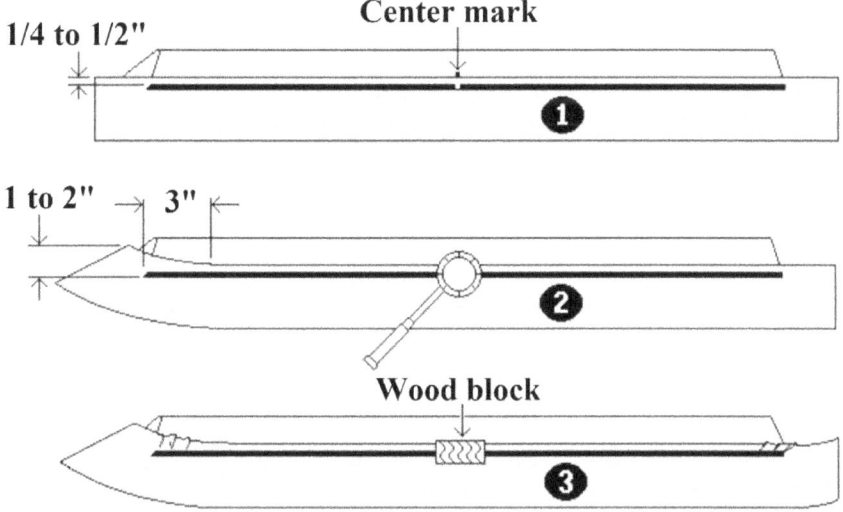

Figure 5-22 *Seating feather strip on side rail.*

End and Side Rails

On the cushion side, carefully trim the excess cloth flush with the top of the feather strip, if there is any. Do not allow the knife to slice the cloth on the top rail side of the feather strip (Figure 5-23).

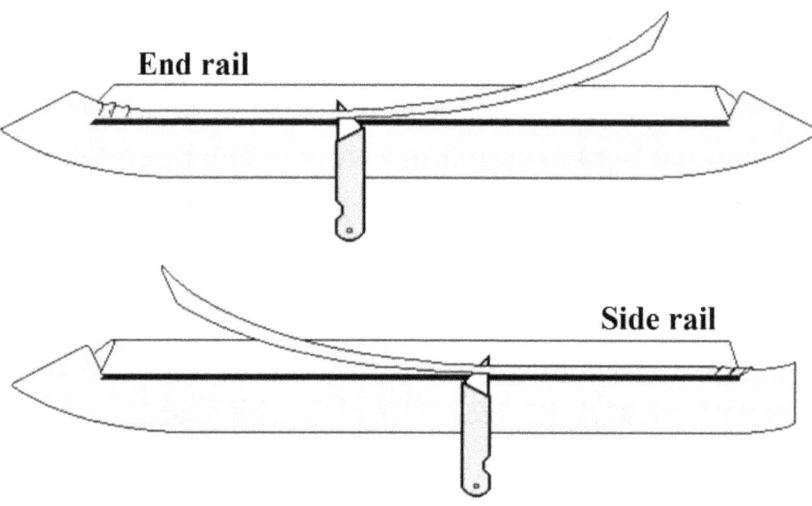

Figure 5-23 *Trim excess cloth.*

Using the block of wood and the rubber mallet, seat the feather strip flush or slightly above the top of the rail, but don't drive it below the top rail. A piece of scrap cloth between the wood block and the top rail will prevent top rail damage and help control feather strip height (Figure 5-24). Ideally, one cloth thickness should remain above the top rail.

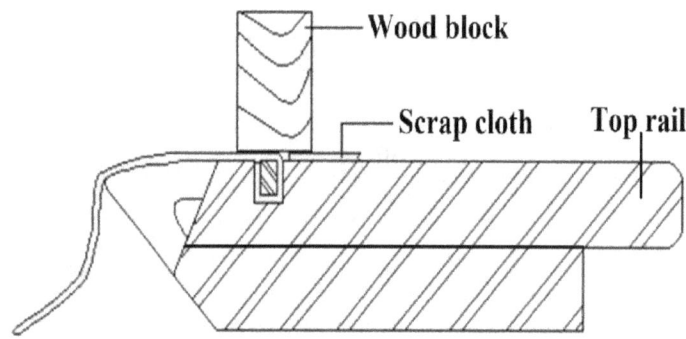

Figure 5-24 *Protect the top rail.*

POOL TABLE ASSEMBLY

Attaching the Rail Cloth

Next, turn the rail face down and pull the rail cloth flat beneath it so the cloth lies on the work surface (Figure 5-25). Make sure old cloth, nails, staples, and other rubbish have been cleared from between the rail cloth and rail. Also, make sure there are no loose staples or other debris remaining on or around the work area that can scratch the top rail or cut the rail cloth.

End Rails

Starting at a corner pocket end, imagine a line running diagonally from the point of the cushion (and facing) to the outside edge of the rail cloth. Also, imagine two more lines running parallel with each edge of the cloth (Figure 5-25).

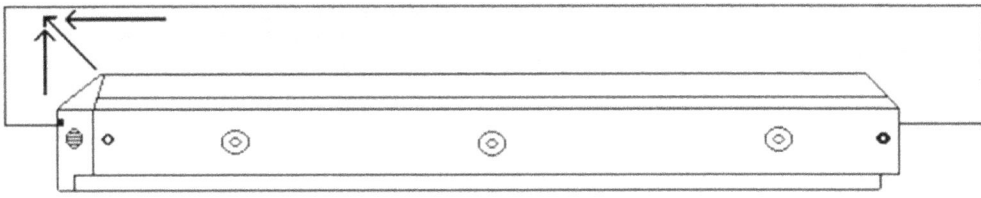

Figure 5-25 *Draw cloth toward its outside corner.*

Where those lines converge at the edge of the cloth, using moderate force, pull the cloth diagonally away from the rail.

Keeping the cloth taut, fold the imaginary lines over the facing, onto the rail bottom, and staple there (Figure 5-26). Pulling the cloth diagonally, as if pulling in three directions at the same time, is important. This helps to eliminate puckers and folds.

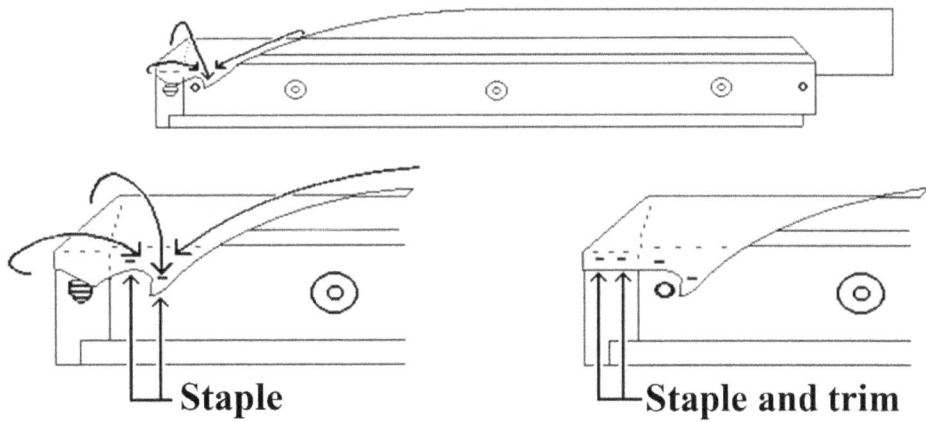

Figure 5-26 *Fold cloth over facing and attach.*

POOL TABLE ASSEMBLY

Next, pull the cloth smoothly across the facing and in little gathers at the bottom of the rail, below the facing. Drive a staple into each gather, and around the perimeter of the facing, so the cloth is held smooth over the facing (Figure 5-26). At first, this may seem difficult but, with patience and a little practice, it can be done.

End rails have two corner pocket ends, so simply repeat the above procedure for the other end (Figure 5-27).

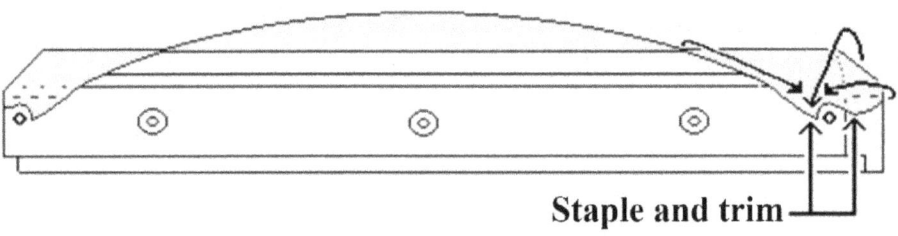

Figure 5-27 *End rails have two corner pocket ends.*

Side Rails

As mentioned earlier, side rails also have a center pocket end, and are therefore treated differently. After following the above procedures for the corner pocket end, pull the cloth in the direction of the center pocket end, wrap it onto the rail bottom, and staple it there (Figure 5-28).

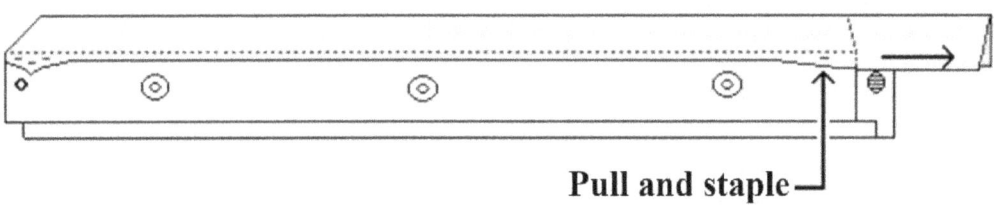

Figure 5-28 *Side rails have corner and center pocket ends.*

To complete the center pocket end, pull the bottom portion of the rail cloth over the facing and staple it there, behind the facing (rail 2 in Figure 5-29).

POOL TABLE ASSEMBLY

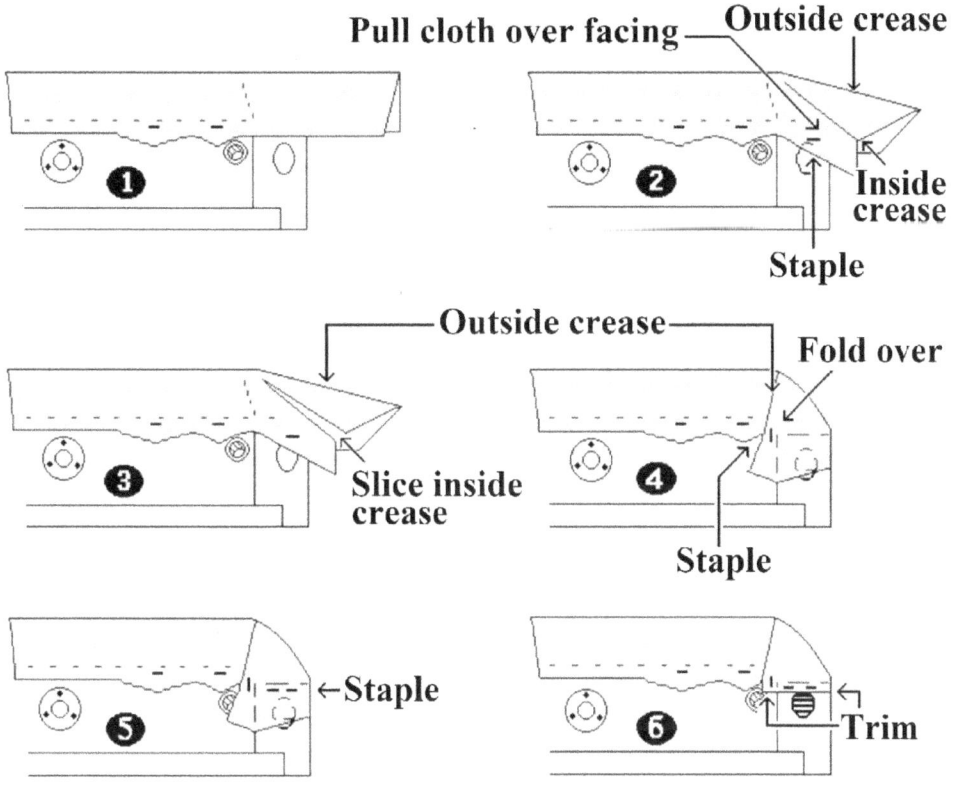

Figure 5-29 *Center pocket fold.*

This makes two creases, one inside, and one outside. Slice the cloth along the inside crease to within 1/4 inch of the facing tip to eliminate that crease (rail 3 in Figure 5-29). Next, keeping the outside crease intact, pull the cloth—and the crease—up and over the facing, onto the bottom of the rail, and staple there. That outside crease should follow the front edge of the facing at the same angle as the cushion (rail 4 in Figure 5-29).

Staple around the back perimeter of the facing while pulling the cloth taut, and do not allow the cloth to pucker on the facing or cushion (rail 5 in Figure 5-29). Trim excess cloth from the back of the facing and bottom of the rail (rail 6 in Figure 5-29).

POOL TABLE ASSEMBLY

Both End and Side Rails

The following instructions are for both end and side rails. At the midpoint, smoothly pull the rail cloth over the bottom of the rail and staple there (rail 1 in Figure 5-30).

Do not pull the cloth so tight that it causes an indentation in the cushion nose, and do not let the cloth pucker on the cushion.

Continue pulling and stapling at approximately 1/2-to-1-inch increments, pulling slightly away from the end and toward the previous staple or tack, until that end of the rail is reached (rail 2 and 3 in Figure 5-30).

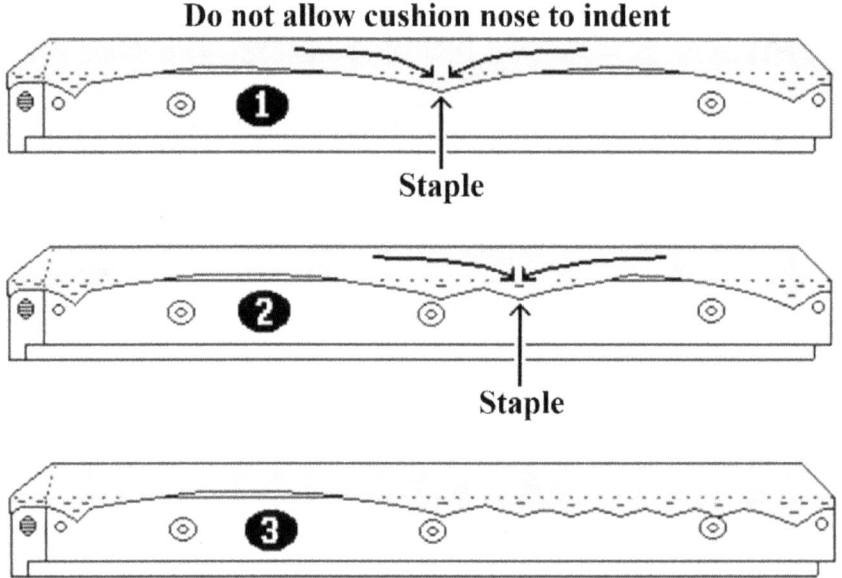

Figure 5-30 *Work from midpoint.*

Some rails have a tacking groove that runs the length of the bottom of the rail. Try to staple within that groove. Staples outside the groove might change the height of the cushion nose when the rails are installed.

-Trick of the Trade-

Pliers can be used to hold and pull the rail cloth; however, they tend to indent the cushion nose inordinately. Use caution.

Repeat to finish the other end of that rail.

Attaching the cloth at 1/2-to-1-inch intervals will usually suffice. However, insert the staples as close to each other as necessary to prevent wrinkling in the rail cloth on any exposed part of the rail. If puckers occur at the bottom of the rail, put a staple in each pucker, so they stay on the bottom of the rail.

Finally, trim all excess cloth from the rail. Trim close to the staples to eliminate the possibility of the cloth wrinkling or folding under the rail when it is installed to the table (Figure 5-31).

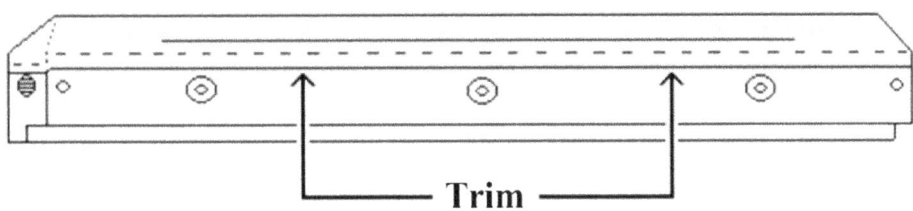

Figure 5-31 *Trim excess cloth.*

POOL TABLE ASSEMBLY

LEVELING THE SLATE

The top of the slates must be aligned flush, with no runoff in relation to each other. The concern is not that the slates are level at this time, but that they are flush with each other and *lying on the same plane*. Once this has been accomplished, the table can be re-leveled as a unit, if necessary.

The best technique to check for slate misalignment is to hold a straightedge across the seam where two slates meet and look beneath it, between it and the slate.

A carpenter's level tilted slightly on edge works fine (Figure 5-32).

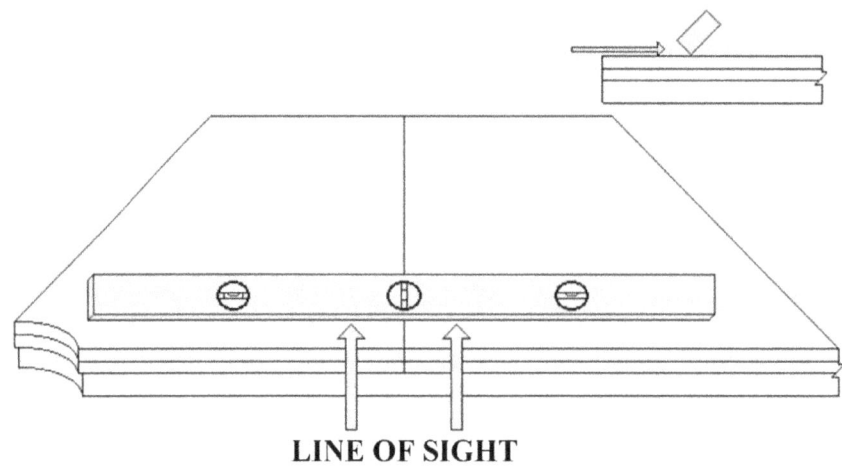

Figure 5-32 *Look between the slate and the carpenter's level.*

If you use a four-foot carpenter's level, look at the position of the seam of two slates at a time, do not try to span all three at once unless you have a longer carpenter's level, say sex feet or more.

Slate height differences or misalignments can be judged by the gap between the straightedge and the slate. Slates must align to within .005 inches (approximately the thickness of a couple sheets of paper) of each other to meet BCA specifications. Although it is not likely to obtain this kind of accuracy along the entire length of the seams, getting it as close as possible by compromising the adjustments along the seam is possible and advisable. Having two positions off by .006 is better than one at .012. Also, these specifications are given here as references only. Measuring each gap or wave along the seam to determine that it is within tolerances is not necessary. Simply peer between the straightedge and the slate and adjust the slate until there is no or little gap between them, and there is no difference between the heights of the two pieces of slate.

A straightedge across a seam will show any one or all of the following four states of alignment or misalignment:

1. The slates will be flush.
2. One slate will be thinner or thicker than the other two.
3. Portions of one or both end slates will be low in relation to the center slate.
4. Some portions of the center slate will be low in relation to the end slate.

Be aware that around the table all states might exist in varying degrees at the same time. It is also possible that correcting one situation will cause one of the others to occur. Also, the seam on one side of a table could be flush while the other side is not. So it is imperative to check, recheck, and correct at least the six positions adjacent to the slate screws along the side and center of both seams shown in Figure 5-33.

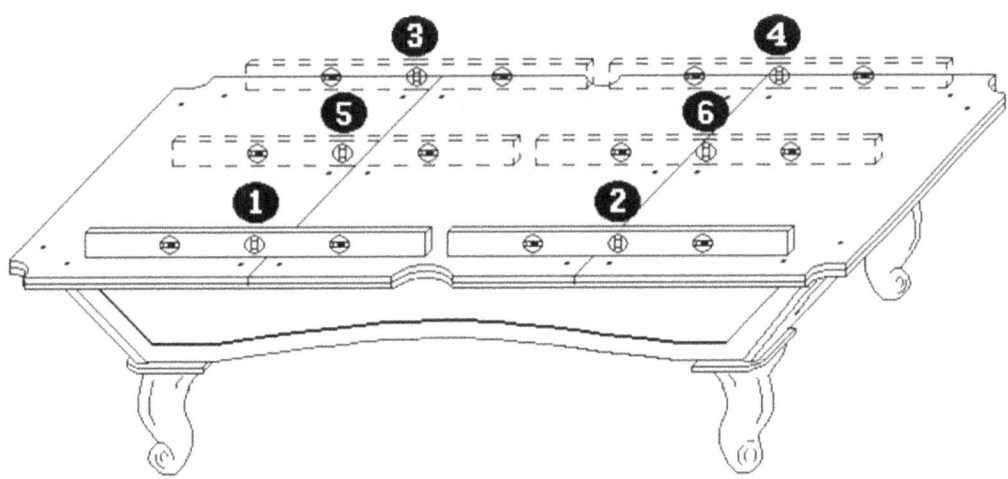

Figure 5-33 *Check at least three positions on each seam.*

To correct for slate misalignment, start with the high slate and lift the low slates to the same height. This is why the slate screws must be tightened first—to decide which is truly the high slate. Shims or wedges are used to raise low slates. Shims can be pieces of thin wood, playing cards, sheet metal, or anything that is flat and thin. However, wedges are much easier to use because of their infinite and minute adjustment possibilities. A few table manufacturers provide slate leveling wedges with their tables, but wedges can also be purchased from most pool table supply stores. Carpenter's door or framing shims (wedges) also work fine and can be purchased from any lumberyard or hardware store. Long, thin, and wide wedges with a gradual taper are superior to short, narrow ones that taper rapidly.

Loosen or remove the slate screws of the low slate and drive a wedge between the slate and the frame to force up the slate. Position the wedge approximately one inch from the seam, close to the slate screw. If the slate board is part of the slate, the wedge must be placed between the slate board and cabinet. If, on the other hand, the slate board is part of the cabinet (slate platform) or no slate board is present, the wedge must be placed directly beneath the slate (Figure 5-34).

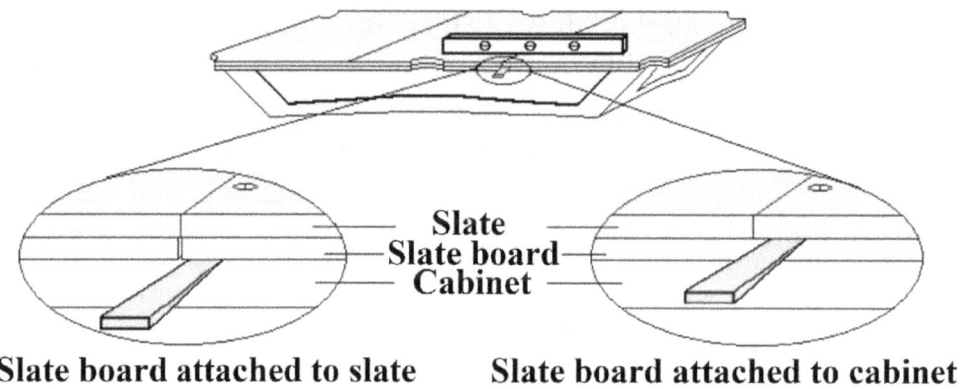

Figure 5-34 *Wedge between the slate and the cabinet.*

If the board beneath the slate is thin or weak and bends downward when wedged, drive the wedges outward from beneath the table where the cabinet will provide more support.

First State

The first of the four states described above is that of complete alignment, however unlikely. This occurs when all six positions along the seams are flush to each other and all three slates are lying on the same plane (Figure 5-35).

-Caution-
Check one side, then the other side, and then the center. It is imperative that the slates are brought flush in some such order. The edges of both seams and all three slates must be flush simultaneously. When the center slate is changed at one seam, it will affect the other seam, so both must be checked and corrected at the same time.

POOL TABLE ASSEMBLY

Figure 5-35 shows positions 1 and 2. Positions 3-4, and 5-6 (Figure 5-33) must also be flush.

When this occurs, simply fill the seams and slate screw holes, and go on with the assembly (see "Filling Slate Seams" on page 43).

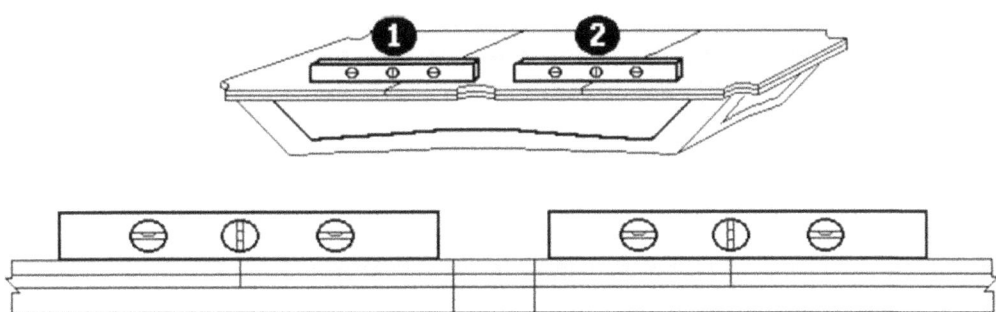

Figure 5-35 *Slates are flush.*

Second State

The second state is one of misalignment and occasionally occurs when a slate or slate board (or portion of the cabinet) is thinner, or thicker, than the others (Figure 5-36).

In this situation, all the screws of that slate must be loosened or removed, and then wedges must be driven beneath each corner of the low slate until it comes up flush with the others.

Figure 5-36 shows positions 1 and 2 only. Positions 3-4, and 5-6 (Figure 5-33) must also be checked and corrected.

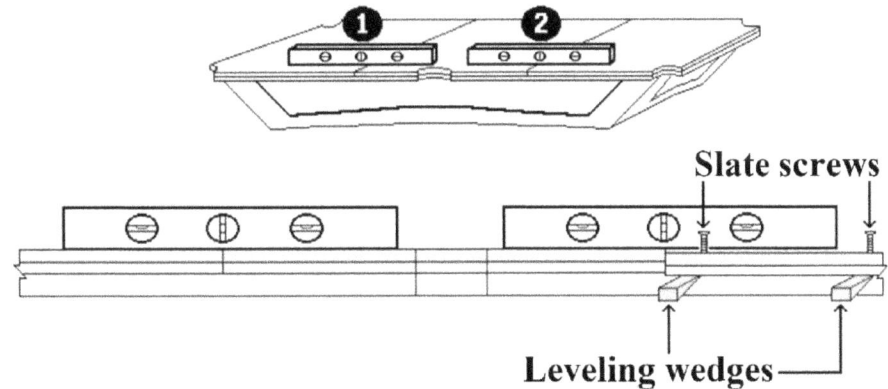

Figure 5-36 *One end slate is low.*

Third State

The third state happens when one or both end slates are lower or pitched toward the ends of the table (Figure 5-37). This generally occurs because the cabinet is bowed.

In this case, loosen or remove the end screws only, and then drive wedges beneath the slate at the low end, or ends, until they are flush with the others.

Figure 5-37 shows positions 1 and 2 only. As before, positions 3-4, and 5-6 (as depicted in Figure 5-33) must also be checked and corrected.

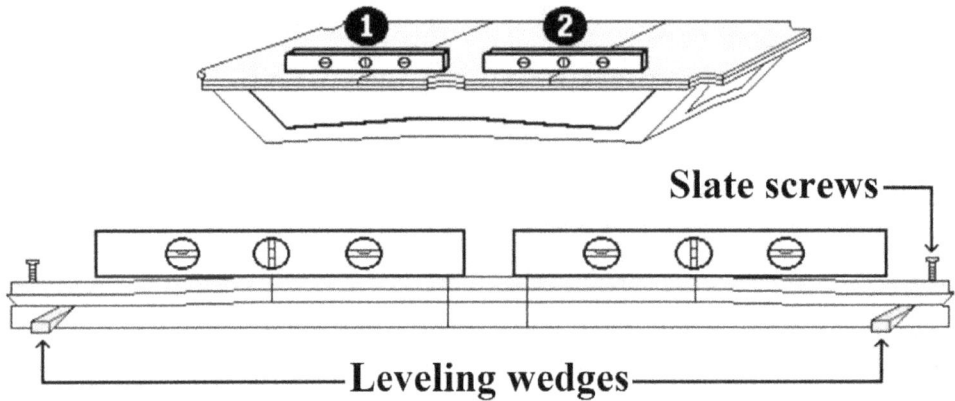

Figure 5-37 *Bowed cabinet.*

Fourth State

The forth state—and the most likely occurrence—is that the center slate will be lower than the ends (Figure 5-38). This usually happens because the center of the cabinet has sagged.

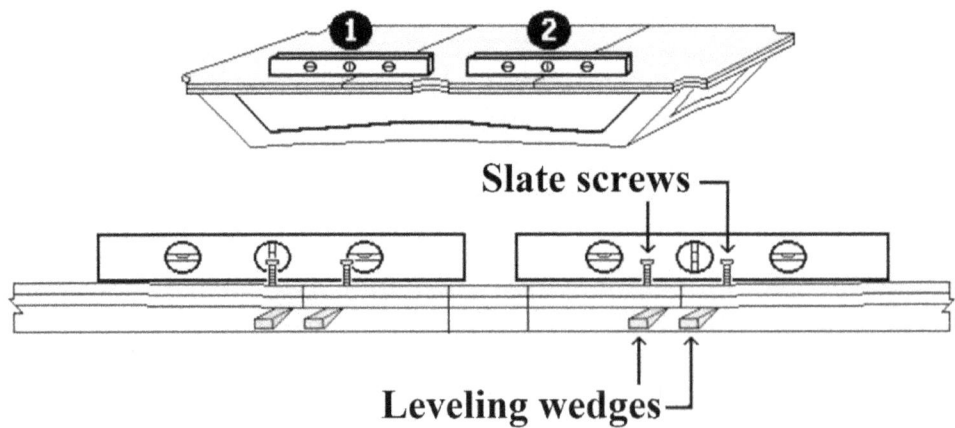

Figure 5-38 *Sagged cabinet.*

In this instance, the end slates will also pitch low toward the center. Loosen the screws along the seams, and drive wedges beneath the center and end slates, at the seams, until all slates are flush with each other.

Figure 5-38 shows positions 1 and 2 only. Also, positions 3-4, and 5-6 (as depicted in Figure 5-35) must also be checked and corrected.

In all the above states of misalignment, as the slates are being wedged flush, tighten the slate screws until they become secure when the slates are flush. If the screws are tightened after the slate is wedged flush the slate will probably be pulled low again. So, tighten and wedge at the same time, in small adjustments.

As mentioned above, level the outside edges of both seams, and then check the center. If the edges are flush but the center is not, loosen the center slate screw of the low slate. Crawl beneath the table and drive a wedge beneath the low slate, next to the slate screw, until it is flush; then tighten the screw.

If no center screws are present, driving a wedge between the slate and the center cross member at the low point can raise a low or sagging slate. However, if a slate is high or bowed, center screws can be added at the center cross member, if you are so inclined. Using a masonry bit, drill the slate and place the screws approximately 1 inch in from the seam's edge to prevent the slate from cracking and chipping.

Wood can bow, warp, shrink, and compress, so do not be too concerned if only one wedge is needed on one corner of a slate while three or more (or none) are used along the opposite side.

Just do what it takes to make the slates flush with each other while sitting on the same plane.

Also, if two corners of the same edge of a slate have been raised, insert another wedge in the middle, between the two corner wedges, to prevent the slate from sagging.

Once the slates are flush, check the overall table to ensure that it is level. Occasionally, especially on carpet, the weight of the slate will cause the cabinet to settle out of level. Re-level the table in the same manner in which the cabinet was leveled initially: find the high end, level it side-to-side, level end-to-end, then level the low end side-to-side.

9 FILLING THE SLATE SEAMS

Imperfections, chips, screw holes, and slate seams can be filled with several materials. The most common three, in order of popularity, are water putty, bees' wax, and auto body filler.

Auto body filler is an excellent and permanent slate seam material. However, it must be mixed, applied, and smoothed quickly because once it dries, expect a considerable amount of sanding, and clean up.

Bees' wax is the most forgiving of the three materials in that it remains soft and usually does not chip, crack, shrink, or become powder. Nevertheless, it is also difficult to apply since it must be melted to a putty consistency, usually with a torch then applied before it hardens again. No sanding is required if the melted wax is smoothed before it dries.

Water putty is the most widely used material for slate seams simply because it is easy to use. It begins as a powder, which is mixed with water to form putty. Water putty dries in a few minutes but allows plenty of time for filling and smoothing. If applied properly, no sanding is required, but it can be easily sanded if needed. Once dry, it is almost as hard as the slate itself.

-Caution-
Do not allow the putty or wax to run through the crack and drip onto the floor.

To use any of the three materials, follow the mixing instructions on their respective containers. Once the material is in a putty state spread it as smooth as possible with a 4-inch putty knife. If the cracks in the seams are large, force some putty about a quarter of an inch into them before wiping it smooth.

Fill all holes, chips, and cracks that will be in the playing area. Those that will lie beneath the rails after they are installed do not have to be filled.

If the slates are not flush and the seam material is "feathered" to fill the difference in height, a slight ball jump will be created. Therefore, if the seam material is spreading in a feathered manner, before it dries, gently drive a wedge beneath the low slate to bring it up to the height of the high slate. Then wipe the seam again with the putty knife so only the crack is filled with seam material. With today's slate, however, eliminating all feathering is not always possible, but keeping it paper-thin is (Figure 5-39).

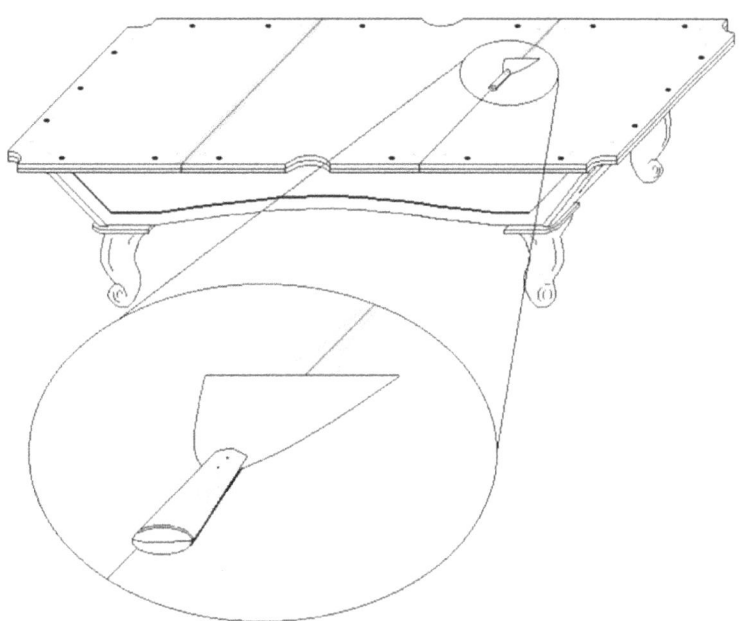

Figure 5-39 *Fill seams and screw holes.*

After the putty dries, use a sandpaper block to smooth out any large humps, bumps, or tool marks, if necessary. This process does not have to be perfect, small imperfections will not be noticed once the cloth is stretched across the slate. Brush all loose debris from the slate, but washing it is not required.

-Trick of the Trade-

If water putty filler is used to fill screw holes, pack the holes with a small amount of dry putty powder first, then spread putty on top of the powder. Once dry, the hardened putty will stay in place, but if it has to be removed later, it will dislodge as a plug with little chipping or drilling required.

POOL TABLE ASSEMBLY

10 INSTALLING THE BED CLOTH

Bed cloth installation is not particularly complicated but can be easily "messed up" if two factors are not remembered. One, pull the cloth as tight as feasible to ensure a smooth, wrinkle free installation, and two, the cloth should be stretched the same in all directions, so the grain or weave is running as straight and square with the table bed as possible.

Make sure the slates are flush and level, and seams, screw holes, chips, etc. are filled.

TABLES WITH BACKED SLATE

Cutout Padding

Cut six strips of cloth, each at a width that equals the thickness of the slate and slate board, and long enough to wrap each pocket cutout. These can usually be taken from the ends of the rail material or the side of the bed cloth. Using contact cement or spray adhesive, glue one strip into each of the six pocket cutouts, about 1/4 inch below the top edge of the slate (Figure 5-40). This will also leave a 1/4-inch overhang at the bottom of the cutout. Slit the overhang in three or four places so it will wrap the slate board for a smooth edge.

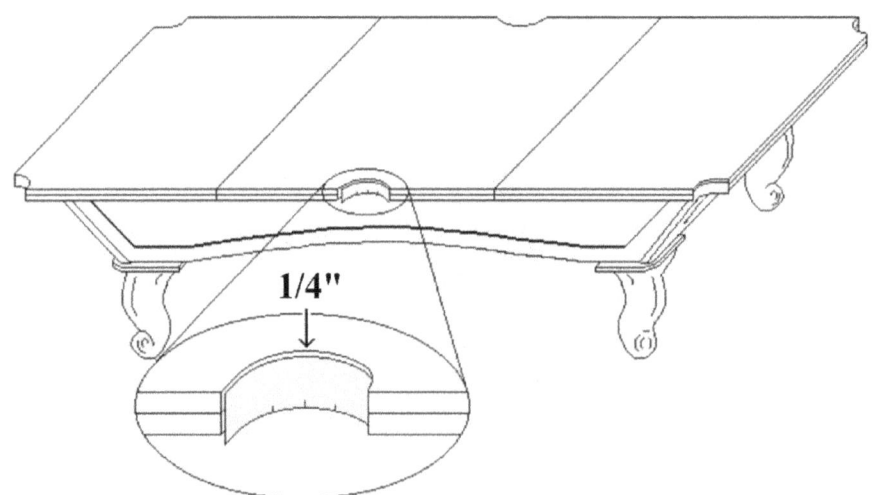

Figure 5-40 *Pocket cutout padding for backed slate tables.*

POOL TABLE ASSEMBLY

Attach Bed Cloth Ends

Next, lay the bed cloth *face up* on the table, leaving an equal amount hanging over each side and end.

Starting at the head of the table, staple the middle of the bed cloth to the slate board, then stretch the cloth toward each side of that end of the table and attach there, staying about 2 inches from the pocket cutouts.

For right now, attach the cloth in only three places: middle and both sides.

Use three or four staples in each area, and crossing or x-ing a couple staples will give them added strength (Figure 5-41).

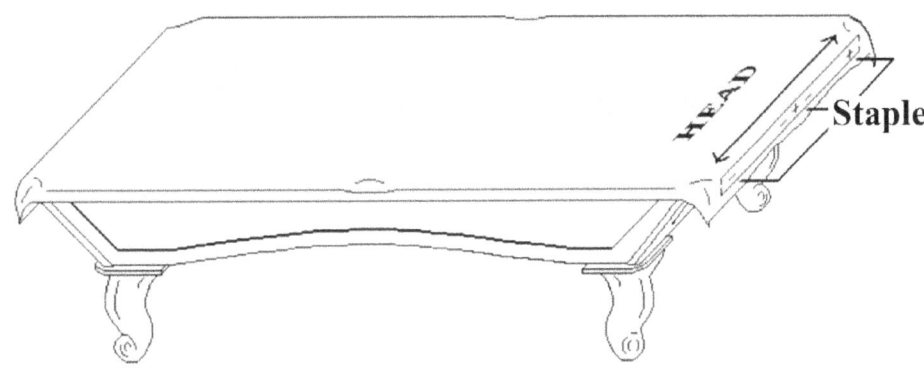

Figure 5-41 *Attach one end first.*

-Caution-
Pliers make stretching easier but can also rip the cloth.
Use them with discretion.

At the foot of the table, using hands or pliers, stretch the middle of the cloth moderately tight and staple (Figure 5-42). Do not let up while attaching. Cloth will begin to loosen almost immediately and over time can become very loose, so keep it pulled tight.

POOL TABLE ASSEMBLY

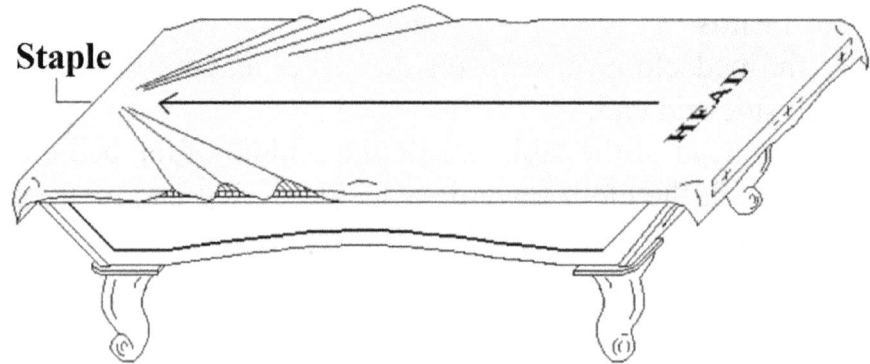

Figure 5-42 *Stretch center to opposite end and attach.*

Next, stretch the cloth toward the sides of that end while pulling from the opposite end and parallel with the side of the table. Stretch the cloth tight and staple the sides of that end staying a couple of inches from the pocket cutouts (Figure 5-43). And, again, middle and both sides only, x-ing the staples for added strength.

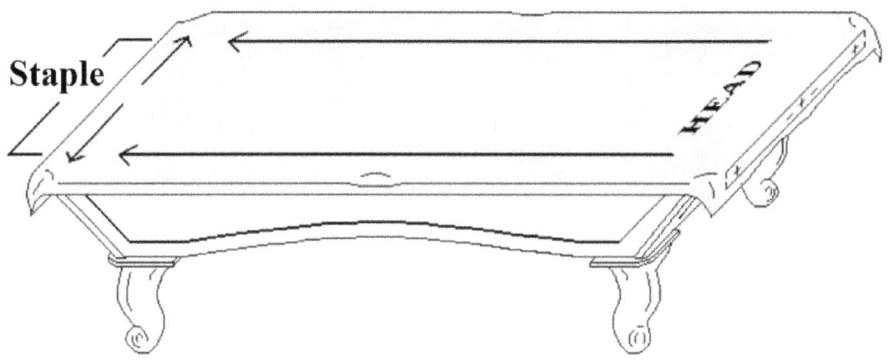

Figure 5-43 *Attach sides of end.*

Attach Center Pocket Cutouts

At either side of the table, stretch the bed cloth into the center pocket cutout and staple at the bottom edge of the slate board (cutout 1 in Figure 5-44). Puckers will occur at the top of the bed, but they will pull out later.

-Caution-
Use care when pulling the tabs, they tend to tear.

Slit the cloth down from the staple, below the slate board (cutout 2 in Figure 5-44), and at two or three other locations, making four to six tabs, each about 1/2 inch wide.

The slits should start at the bottom edge of the slate board so that neither the slate nor the slate board will show. If this proves to be impossible, let the slits extend upward into the cutout, but not by more than 1/2 inch.

When the slits extend into the cutouts, the padding strips glued there earlier will hide the slate and slate board, producing a fairly neat pocket cutout. Pull the cloth smooth around the face of the cutout and attach the tabs below the cutout.

Staple the middle two tabs first (cutout 3 in Figure 5-44), then work from the outside toward the middle to eliminate the puckers in the cutout face (cutouts 4 and 5 in Figure 5-44).

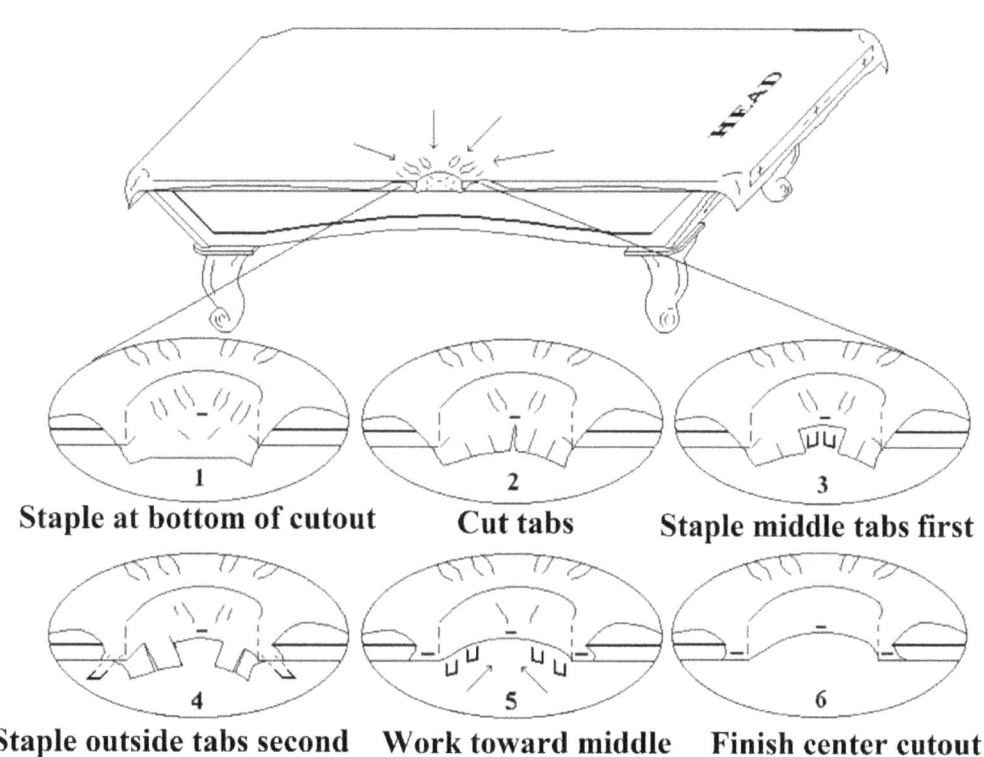

1. Staple at bottom of cutout
2. Cut tabs
3. Staple middle tabs first
4. Staple outside tabs second
5. Work toward middle
6. Finish center cutout

Figure 5-44 *Attach first center pocket cutout.*

POOL TABLE ASSEMBLY

In some cases it may be necessary to work from the middle toward the outside, just do whichever works better for you. Again, do not worry about the puckers on top; they should pull out later (cutout 6 in Figure 5-44). At the other side of the table, repeat the process for the second center pocket cutout.

Attach Corner Pocket Cutouts

For the corner pocket cutouts, start at any of the four and draw the cloth along that side, toward the corner pocket cutout and away from the opposing center pocket, and attach an inch or two from that cutout. The cloth will pull slightly from across the table, but most of it will come from the center pocket of that side and should be pulled tight enough to eliminate puckers on top of the bed, at that side of the center pocket of that side (Figure 5-45).

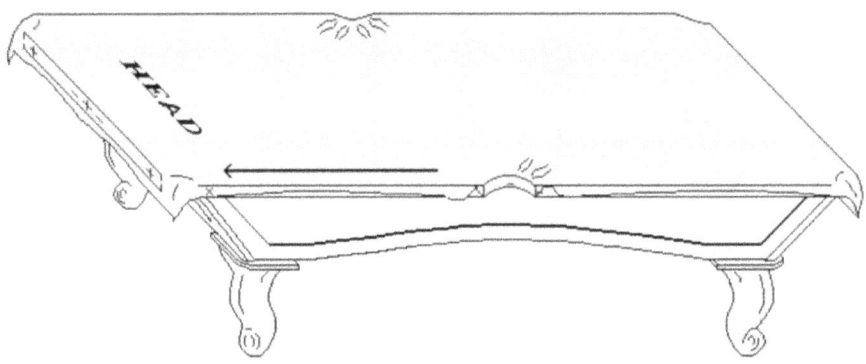

Figure 5-45 *Attach sides at corner cutout.*

Staple the cloth with three or four staples, crossing them for strength, if necessary. Repeat the process for the remaining three corner cutouts.

To finish the corner pocket cutouts, stretch the cloth into the cutout and attach at the bottom of the slate board (cutout 1 in Figure 5-46)

You may get a small pucker or "bubble" at the top of the cutout. This bubble should pull out when the outside taps are attached.

Slit the cloth down from the staple, below the slate board, and at two or three other locations around the cutout to make four to six tabs, again each tab should be about 1/2 inch wide (cutout 2 in Figure 5-46). The slits should start at the bottom edge of the slate board so that neither the slate nor the slate board will show. If this proves to be impossible, try not to let the slits extend more than ½ inch onto the cutout.

POOL TABLE ASSEMBLY

When the slits extend into the cutouts, the padding strips glued there earlier will hide the slate and slate board, producing an acceptable pocket cutout.

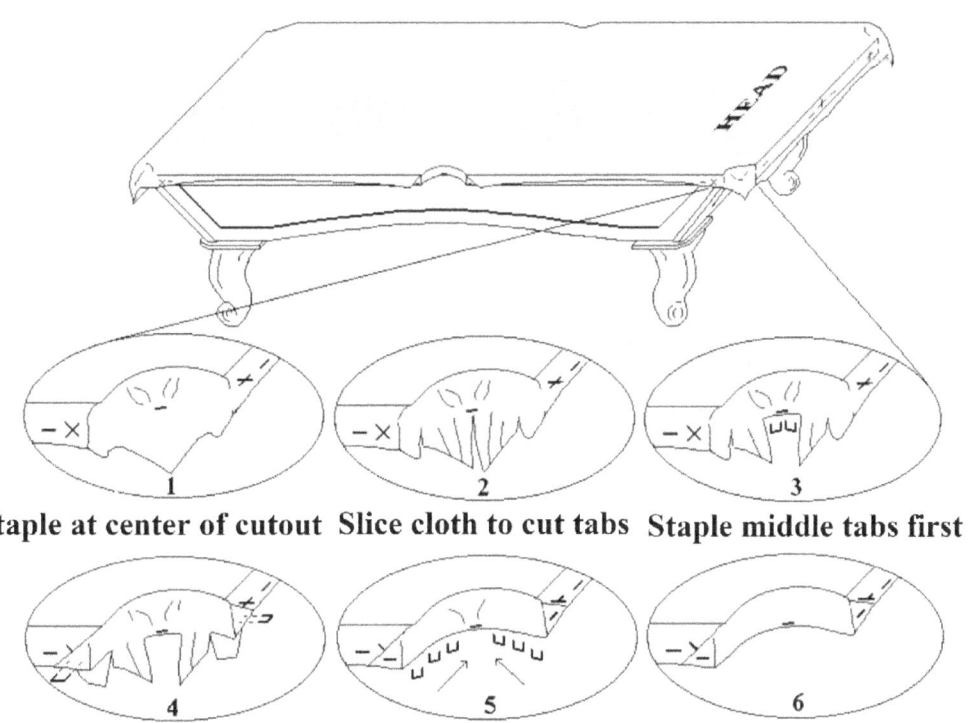

Figure 5-46 *Attach corner pocket cutouts.*

Pull the cloth smooth around the face of the cutout and staple the tabs below the cutout. Staple the middle two tabs first (cutout 3 in Figure 5-46), then work from the outside toward the middle to eliminate any puckers at the top or within the cutout face (cutouts 4 and 5 in Figure 5-46). The finished corner should be smooth (cutout 6 in Figure 5-46). Repeat the process for the other three corner pocket cutouts.

POOL TABLE ASSEMBLY

Attach Sides and Ends

Next, stretch the cloth and staple along one side and then the other, stapling every three to four inches. When you do the second side, pull the cloth as tight as possible. Now, stretch and staple the ends (Figure 5-47).

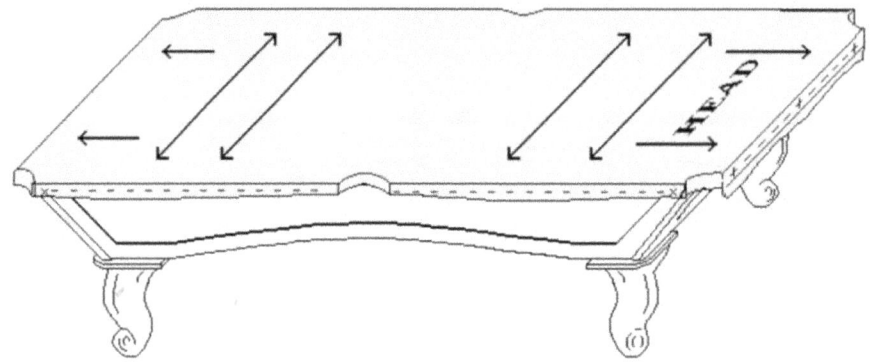

Figure 5-47 *Finish attaching sides and ends.*

TABLES WITH UNBACKED SLATE

Some tables with unbacked slate have slate platforms that extend to the edge of the slate and double as slate backing boards. That is, the bed cloth is stapled to the platform.

Other unbacked slate tables have a narrow, more rigid slate platform that does not extend to the edge of the slate (Figure 5-48). The purpose of these narrow platforms is to solidly hold the slate in place; therefore, the bed cloth must be *glued* directly onto the edge of the slate.

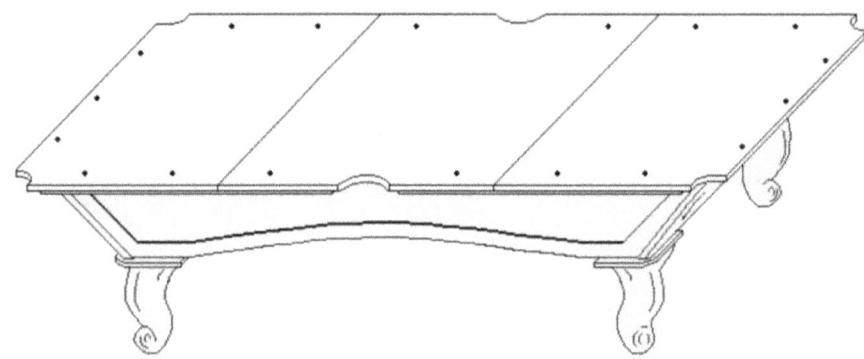

Figure 5-48 *Three-piece unbacked slate tables.*

55

POOL TABLE ASSEMBLY

Glue and Attach One End

Lay the bed cloth face up on the table, leaving an equal amount hanging over each side and end.

If possible, cover the cabinet with paper, cardboard, or a drop cloth to prevent glue over spray from settling on it. And newspaper, cardboard, or some similar material spread on top of the bed cloth will also protect it from overspray. Fold 8 to 10 inches of one end of the cloth up so the underside shows (Figure 5-49).

-Trick of the Trade-

Light over spray can usually be peeled off with the sticky side of masking or strapping tape. Persistent overspray can be removed with mineral spirits.

Use spray adhesive like 3M brand 77 or 76, or brushable contact cement. All three adhere fine but spray adhesive is the easiest to work with, and 76 withstands high temperatures like summertime garages and so forth. Spray (or brush) a 2-inch band of glue the full width of the edge of that end of the slate along the top and bottom (Figure 5-49).

Also, apply a band of glue approximately 4 inches wide along the width of the underside of the bed cloth. Allow all surfaces to become tacky according to specific glue manufactures instructions, usually two to five minutes.

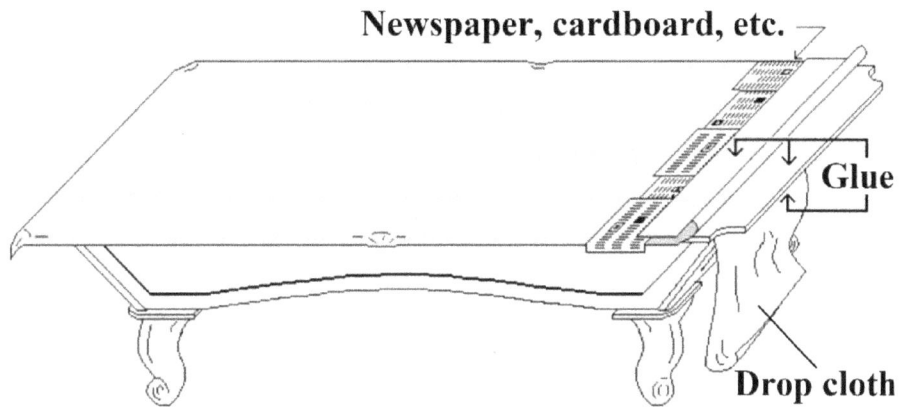

Figure 5-49 *Apply glue to slate and cloth.*

Unfold the cloth and attach the *middle of that end* to the top and edge of the slate, letting the cloth overhang, but do not attach the bottom at this time. Stretch the cloth toward each side of that end of the slate and attach, keeping the cloth edge parallel with the edge of the slate (Figure 5-50).

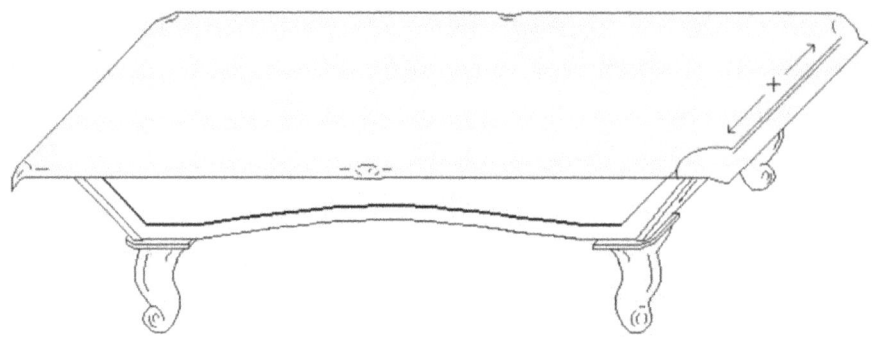

Figure 5-50 *Attach middle then stretch to sides.*

From the bottom of the slate, at the pocket cutouts, cut the overhanging cloth at a 45-degree angle down and in. This prevents any excess from wrapping into the pocket cutout.

After cutting the angle, fold the overhanging cloth under the slate and attach it to the bottom, but do not allow the cloth to pucker or crease beneath the slate; it should be smooth to ensure a good grip (Figure 5-51).

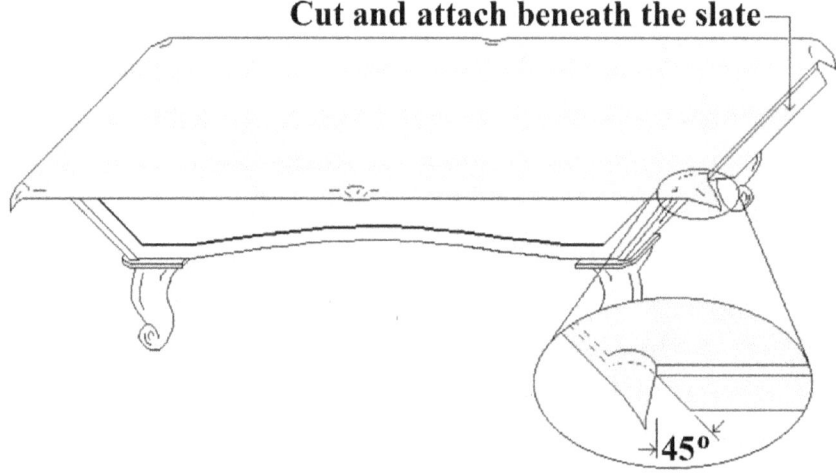

Figure 5-51 *Attach first end.*

POOL TABLE ASSEMBLY

-Caution-
Some manufacturers and mechanics glue only the top and edge, while others glue only the bottom and edge. However, it will not harm the table to glue all three surfaces—2" of the top, edge, and 2" of the bottom—to ensure that the cloth holds.

Glue and Attach Second End

Protect the other end of the table with a drop cloth, or some such material, and then apply glue to it in the same manner as the first end—edges of slate, approximately 2 inches on top and bottom, and approximately 4 inches along the width of the underside of the cloth (refer back to Figure 5-49).

After the glue has become tacky, stretch the middle tight to that end and attach the top and edge (Figure 5-52). Keep the cloth taut while attaching. Cloth will begin to loosen almost immediately, and over time can become very loose, so it needs to be tight and smooth now.

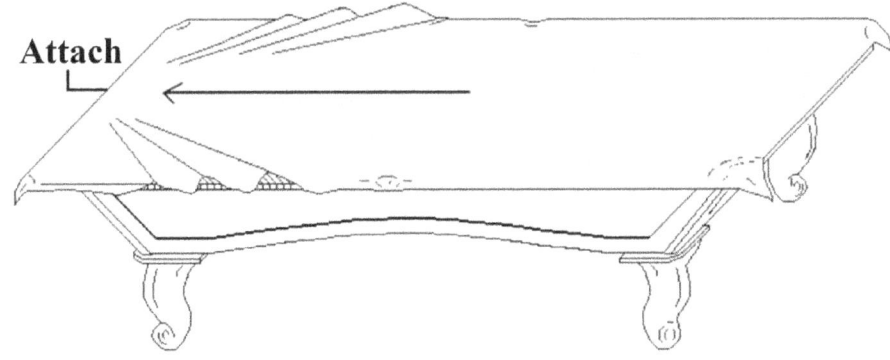

Figure 5-52 *Stretch center and attach.*

Next, stretch the cloth toward the sides of that end, pulling parallel with the side of the slate and from the opposite end of the table, and attach to the top and edge of the slate. Again, stretch the cloth tight and smooth while attaching to the top and edge of the slate (Figure 5-53).

POOL TABLE ASSEMBLY

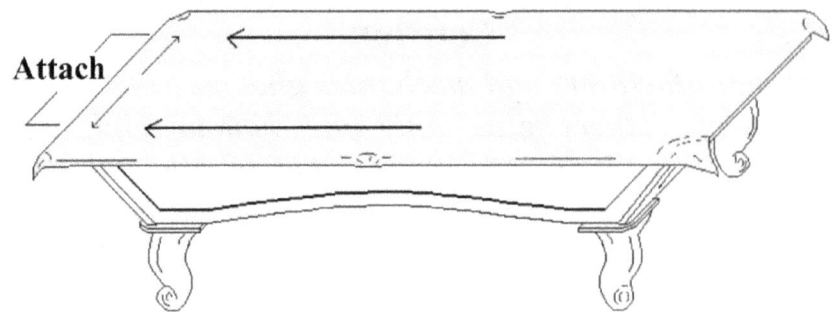

Figure 5-53 *Stretch parallel with slate and attach.*

As before, cut the overhanging cloth at a 45-degree angle from the pocket cutouts before attaching beneath the slate (refer back to Figure 5-51), and as before, do not let the cloth pucker or crease beneath the slate.

Glue and Attach One Side

Protect one side of the table with a drop cloth material. Fold 8 to 10 inches of cloth of that side up to expose the underside. Use newspaper, cardboard, drop cloth etc. to protect the top of the cloth from spray. Apply glue to the slate and the underside of the cloth as before. This time include the pocket cutouts in the gluing process (Figure 5-54).

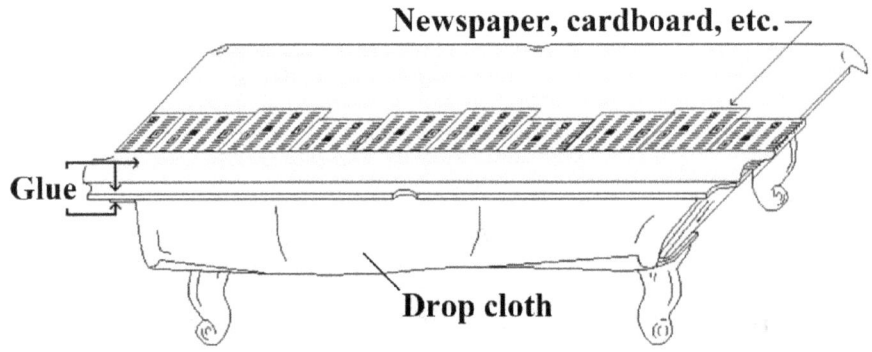

Figure 5-54 *Apply glue to slate and cloth.*

Unfold the cloth and stretch it along that side of the slate, from one end toward the other, and attach the ends, next to the corner pocket cutouts—top and edge only.

59

POOL TABLE ASSEMBLY

Allow the cloth to pucker slightly in the corner pocket cutouts. Attach the remainder of that side, keeping the edge of the cloth parallel with the slate. Cut the overhang at a 45-degree angle from the pocket cutouts then attach to the bottom of the slate (Figure 5-55).

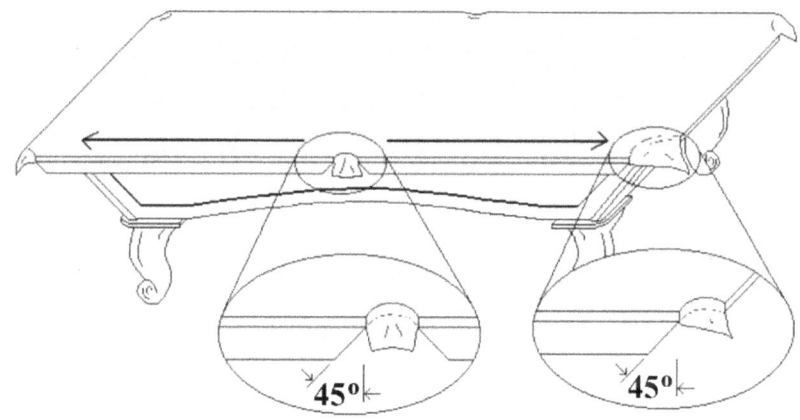

Figure 5-55 *Attach first side and cut overhang angle.*

Glue and Attach Second Side

Glue the other side (refer back to Figure 5-54 and do not forget the drop cloth, etc.). Stretch the bed cloth along that side, first one end, and then the other. This time, however, pull the cloth from across the slate at the same time. Stretch it as tight as possible, try to get a slight pucker in the corner pocket cutouts, and attach only to the top and edges of the slate (Figure 5-56). Cut the overhang at a 45-degree angle from the pocket cutouts, and then attach it to the bottom of the slate.

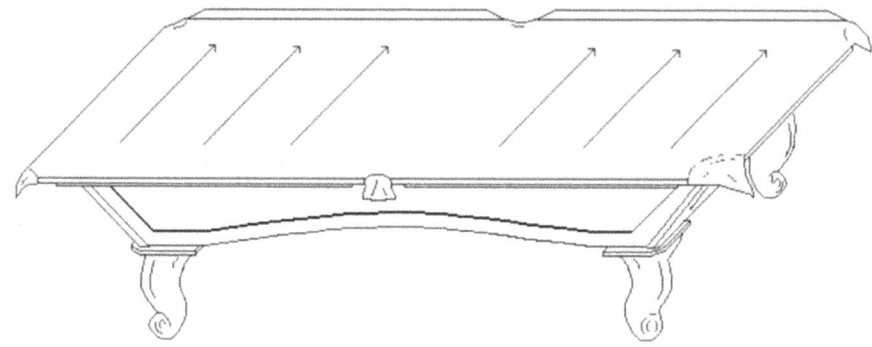

Figure 5-56 *Attach the other side.*

POOL TABLE ASSEMBLY

Glue and Attach Pocket Cutouts

To finish, slit the cloth in the pocket cutouts to make four to six tabs depending on the curvature of the cutout—the smaller the radius the more tabs. Try to prevent the slits from extending up past the bottom of the slate. If they do, keep them between a quarter to one-half the thickness of the slate.

-Trick of the Trade-

Strapping tape on the bottom surface of the slate, across all the tabs, will help prevent them from slipping.

Pull each tab tight and attach to the slate edge and bottom (Figure 5-57).

Although not necessary, but for appearance, the use of pocket cutout padding (see Figure 5-40) up to half the thickness of the slate may be used behind the tabs to hide the slate and, if used, should be installed before the tabs are attached; however, the gluing surface used for the padding could be crucial in holding the tabs in place.

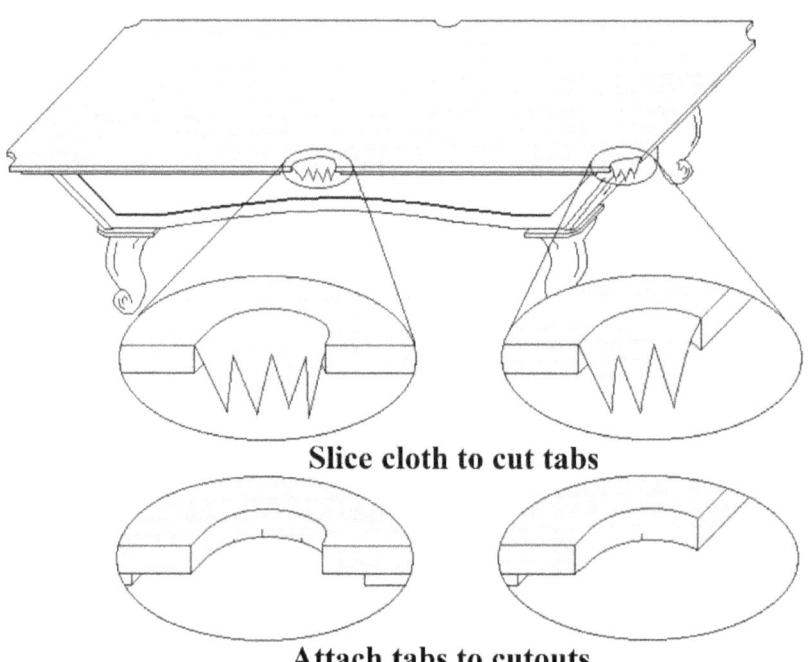

Figure 5-57 *Cut pocket cutout tabs.*

POOL TABLE ASSEMBLY

INSTALLING THE RAILS AND POCKETS

Trim and Cut Bolt Holes

On *backed* slate tables, trim the excess cloth along the bottom edge of the slate board, below the staples, and reinforce any staple that appears not to be holding by driving another beside it.

On all tables, using a utility knife or scissors cut rail-bolt holes in the bed cloth (Figure 5-58). Without cutting these holes, it is difficult, if not impossible, to later find the rail lugs when attaching the rails. Locate the holes from beneath the slate to guarantee cutting only rail-bolt holes.

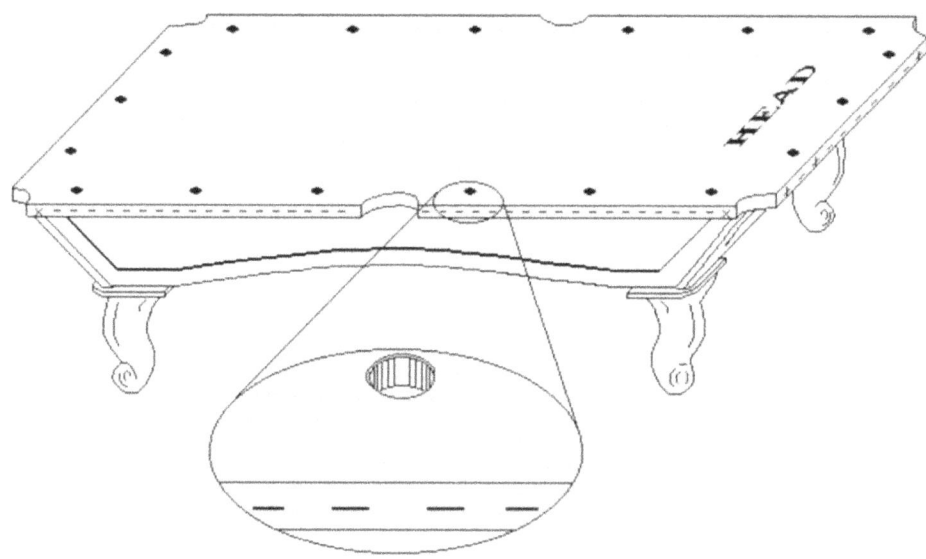

Figure 5-58 *Trim edges and cut rail bolt holes.*

Tables with Corner Castings

Tables with plastic or metal corner rail castings have plastic interior pockets (see page 66) that are installed after the rails have been assembled. The corner (and often side) castings are usually attached to the rails in much the same way as are leather pockets, simply attach them and proceed to the following instructions. Aprons for these tables are generally attached by screws into the rails and are joined by plastic or metal corner trim.

Aprons

Aprons are often permanently and securely attached to the rail at the factory (Figure 5-59) and, therefore, do not need any assembly.

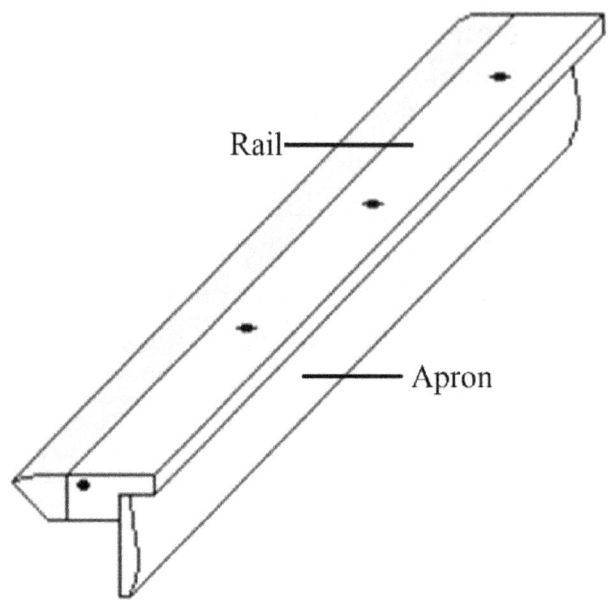

Figure 5-59 *Apron permanently attached to the rail.*

Some aprons come separated from the rails and must be attached to them before they are assembled onto the table. The flat bracket style of attachment, for instance, must be fastened to the rails while they are upside down (Figure 5-59).

The two end aprons are an inch or two longer than the four side aprons, to match the length of the end rails.

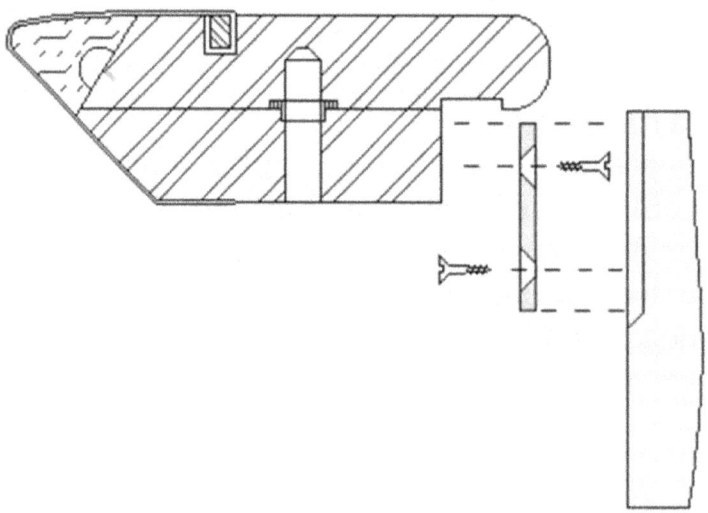

Figure 5-60 *Install flat-bracket aprons before attaching rails.*

POOL TABLE ASSEMBLY

All the other aprons are installed after the rails are bolted down and usually after the pocket webbing has been affixed to the slate board.

Attach them with the provided angle brackets, wood blocks, exposed screws that pass through the face, or some combination (Figure 5-61).

The two end aprons are an inch or two longer than the four side aprons and are interchangeable. The four side aprons are often interchangeable on a cater-corner basis only.

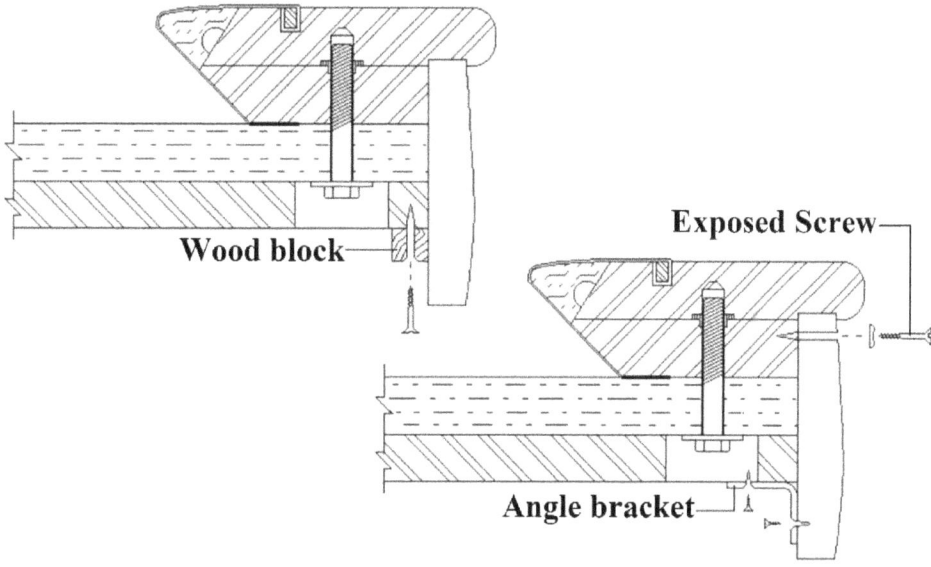

Figure 5-61 *Install these aprons after attaching rails.*

Rails

Installing rails is relatively straightforward. However, some procedures should be considered in advance to make the job easier. The following instructions give insight into those procedures.

A standard system of identifying the rails is to call the head rail and the foot rail END RAILS, then standing at either end of the table the side rail on the right is called a RIGHT RAIL and the side rail on the left is called a LEFT RAIL. End rails are an inch or so longer than the side rails, and side rails have a corner pocket angle and a side pocket angle (see Figure 5-20 on page 29).

POOL TABLE ASSEMBLY

End rails are interchangeable with each other; right rails are interchangeable with each other; and left rails are interchangeable with each other (Figure 5-62).

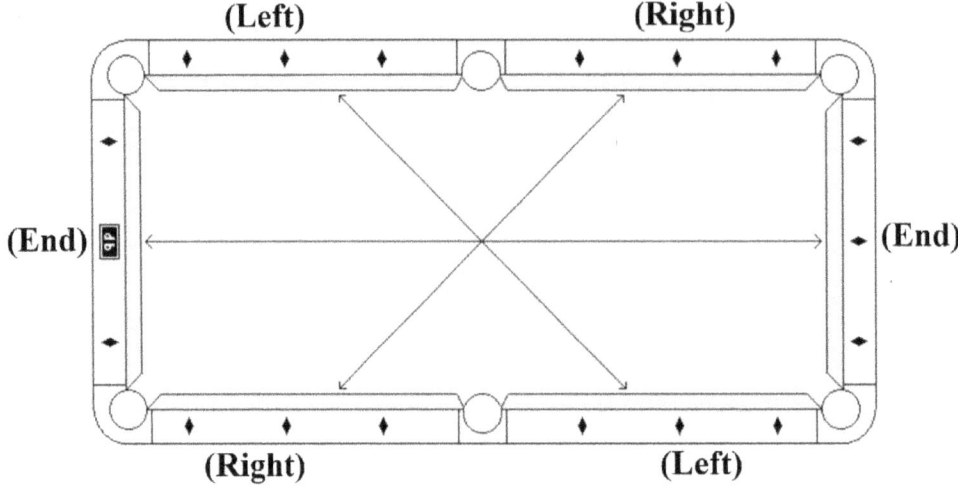

Figure 5-62 *Interchangeable rails.*

Pockets

Pockets are attached to the rails by pocket lugs that are inserted into the holes at the end of the rails. Pocket lugs are drilled and tapped and are attached to the rail by bolts that penetrate the rail from the bottom (Figure 5-63).

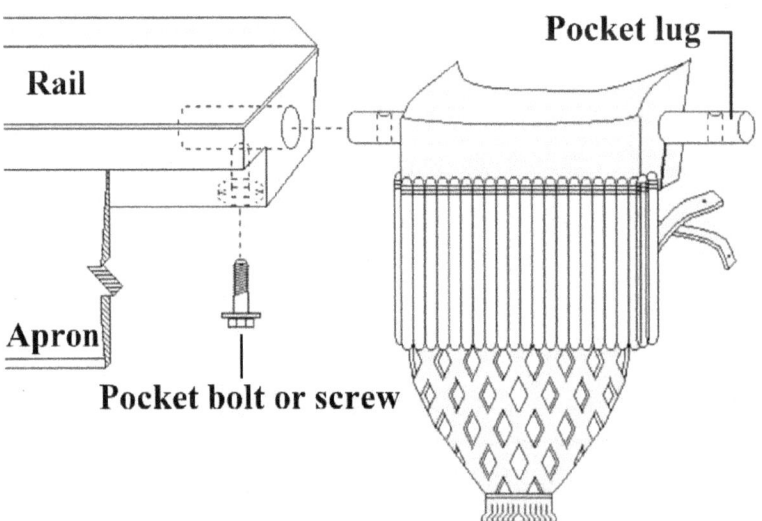

Figure 5-63 *Number 6 iron lugs.*

POOL TABLE ASSEMBLY

Pockets with shields (instead of fringe) often come with Velcro tabs to help keep the shield straight and flat. Simply attach the Velcro to the backside of the apron then attach the tabs to the Velcro (Figure 5-64).

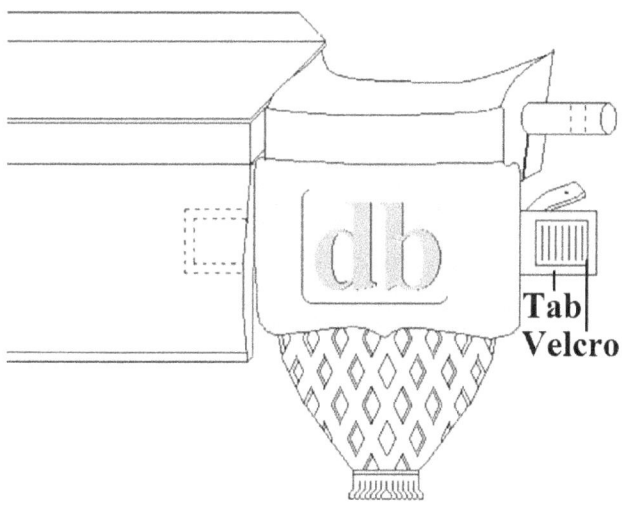

Figure 5-64 *Pockets with shields and tabs.*

Leather pockets (or metal rail castings) are usually assembled onto the rails before the rails are attached to the table.

This can be done by working from under the table with the rails in their usual upright position, but hanging over the edge of the table so the pocket bolts can be reached.

-Caution-
Do not bolt all six rails and pockets together and try to turn the whole unit over as one assembly. The points of connection between the center pockets and rails are far too weak for such a maneuver. Also, for the same reason, do not transport the rails in this configuration.

POOL TABLE ASSEMBLY

However, assembling the rails and pockets upside-down on the table is much easier. Construct two horseshoe assemblies. One assembly consists of an end rail, two side rails, and two corner pockets.

The other is the same except that the two center pockets are added to the side rails (Figure 5-65). Make sure the pockets are snug against the rail ends before the pocket bolts are tightened. If a space is left between a pocket and top rail, the assembly will be weak, and the gap will look unfinished once the table is completed. As the bolts are tightened, the back of the pocket may raise 0 to 5 degrees higher than the front to ensure that the pocket iron forces the ball down into the pocket.

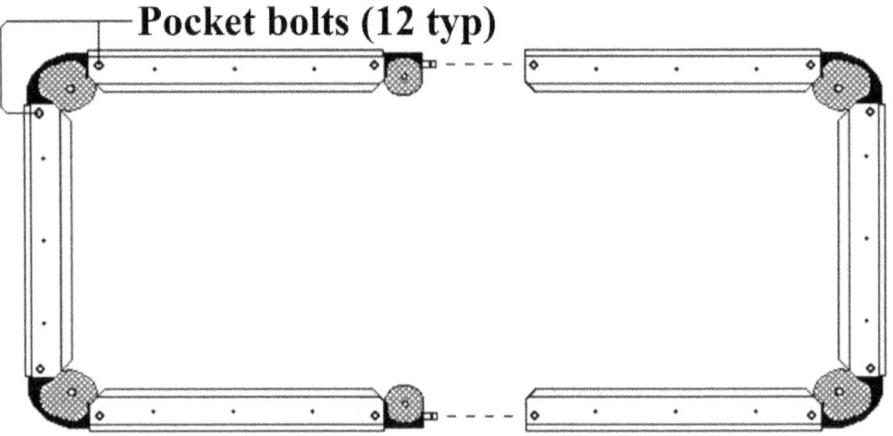

Figure 5-65 *Assemble rails and pockets upside down.*

Assembling The Rails

The two assemblies are then turned over and positioned on the table. Turning each assembly right-side up can be awkward and could put undue stress on the pocket irons and rails if care is not taken. However, two people can turn the assembly with ease.

Once the two assemblies have been righted, insert the remaining two center pocket lugs into their respective side rails and screw in the last two pocket bolts from beneath.

Now, start all rail bolts, but do not tighten, the rail must be aligned and squared first (Figure 5-66).

67

POOL TABLE ASSEMBLY

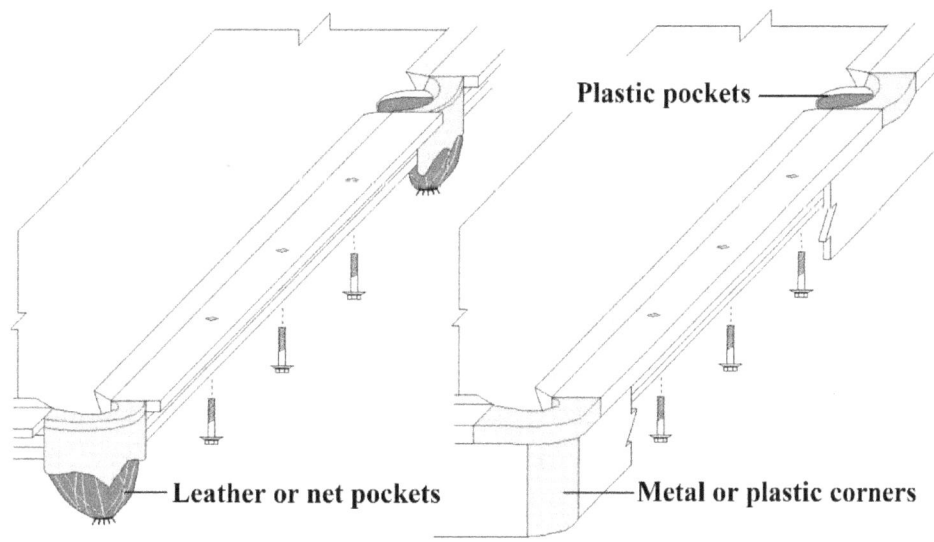

Figure 5-66 *Start all rail bolts.*

Next, check to ensure that all pockets or pocket openings align with their respective pocket cutouts by looking down into each pocket. The rail assembly can be repositioned and aligned as much as needed before the rail bolts are tightened.

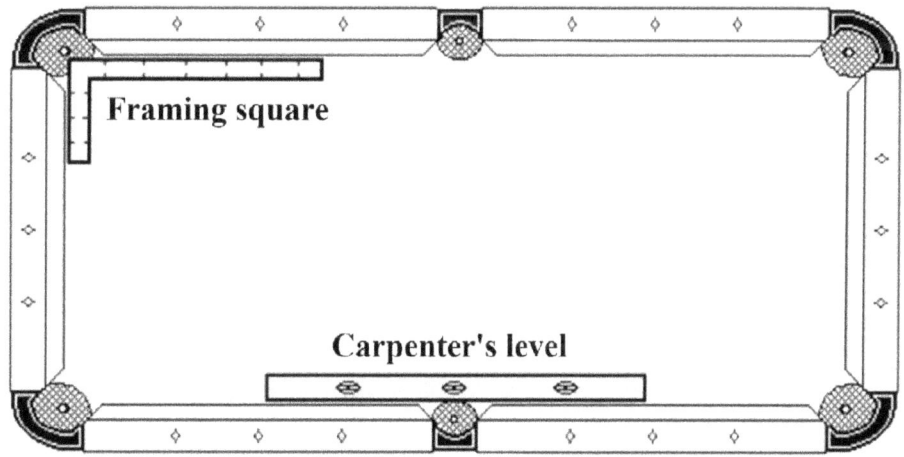

Figure 5-67 *Square and align rails.*

POOL TABLE ASSEMBLY

Use a carpenter's framing square to square the corners, and the straight edge of a carpenter's level to align the side rails with each other (Figure 5-67).

After the rails have been squared, aligned, and straightened, tighten all rail bolts.

Attaching Leather Pocket Webbing

Fasten the pocket webbing to the bottom of the slate board or platform. This can be done with 3/8- or 1/2-inch staples, or 3/4-inch nails or screws. Evenly spread the webbing tabs under the slate board and attach them there, beneath the table (Figure 5-68). Some new style pockets are made with tabs connected to each other. Sometimes this can make screwing them to the slate board easier, but usually they must be separated so they can be evenly spaced around the pocket cutout.

Inside each leather pocket is a trim sheathing. Each end of this sheathing is usually folded or cut straight down, following the contour of the back of the rail into the pocket, and then nailed to the end of the rail to make a neat looking pocket area (Figure 5-68).

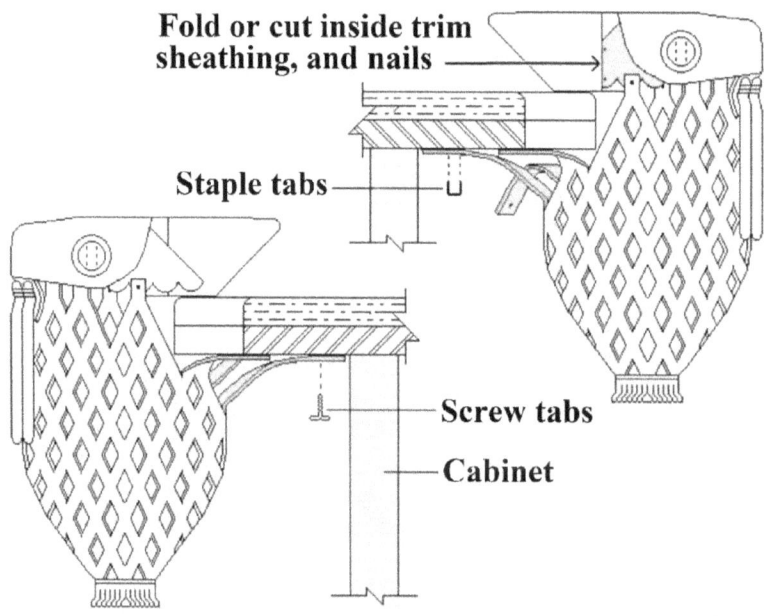

Figure 5-68 *Attach webbing tabs to bottom of slate board.*

POOL TABLE ASSEMBLY

After the webbing is attached, install the aprons as shown on pages 59 and 60, (Figures 5-60 and 61), if needed.

Attaching Plastic Pockets

Plastic pockets are inserted into the pocket cutout from beneath the table, after the rails are assembled. Some tables have smaller pockets cutouts than standard. In these cases, the pockets must be trimmed to fit. Usually, though, only the center pocket needs to be trimmed.

To trim, center the pocket within the cutout, then, using a scribe (or pencil) mark a line from the top edge of the pocket flange, where the rail cloth meets the top rail, down to the top of the pocket basket (pocket 1 in Figure 5-69).

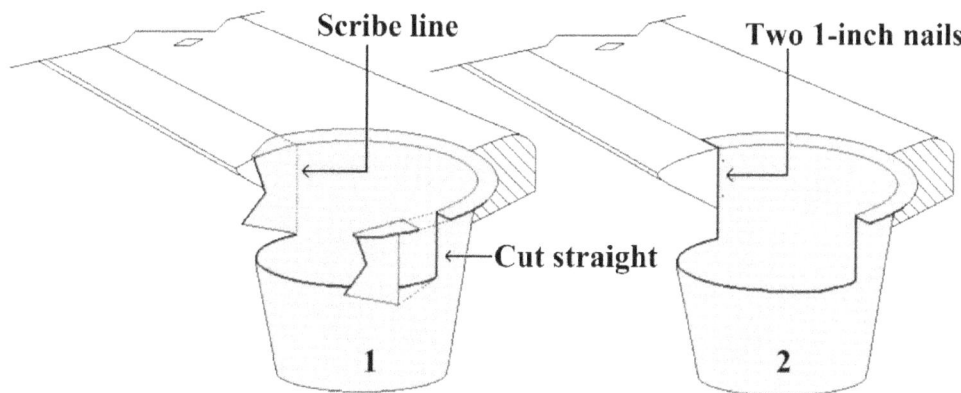

Figure 5-69 *Nail pocket trim sheathing.*

Remove the pocket and trim (cut) along the marked line. Reinsert the pocket into position and nail it to the rail.

Two 1-inch nails placed slightly behind the rail facing will be sufficient (pocket 2 in Figure 5-69), although one at the back of the pocket can be used to keep the pocket solid, if desired. The nails do not need to be any larger than one inch.

POOL TABLE ASSEMBLY

Playing Field Layout

The spot itself is normally pre-manufactured and attached to the playing field with pre-applied adhesive but can be drawn on with a pencil or felt-tip pen.

-Trick of the Trade-

Although a head spot is not necessary on a pool table, if marked, it can be used to easily locate the head string or to allow the choice of breaking from either end to increase the life of the billiard cloth.

The foot string is a line a quarter the length of the playing field at the foot end and aligns with the center sights of the side rails.

The long string is a line that divides the width of the playing field in half. It aligns with the center sights of the head and foot rails—the two end rails (Figure 5-70).

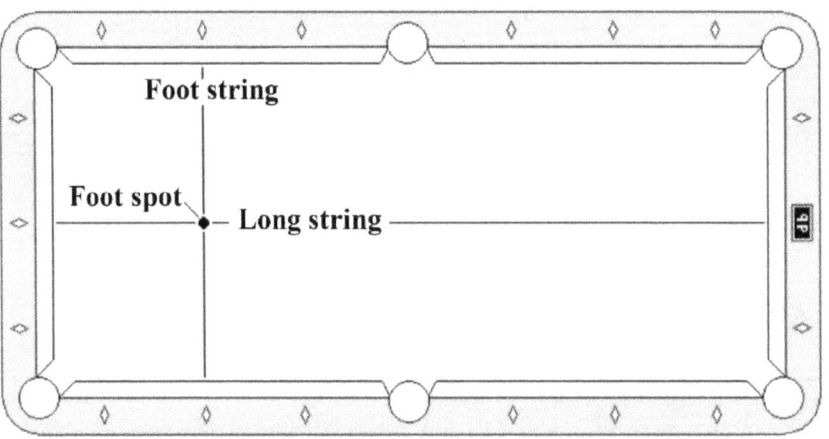

Figure 5-70 *Pool table foot spot location.*

The foot spot is located where the foot string intersects with the long string. This is the spot at which the apex of the triangle of balls is racked. Generally, only the foot spot is marked, and string lines are usually considered imaginary lines and are not drawn.

Congratulations.
You now have a pool table, and you did it yourself!

POOL TABLE ASSEMBLY

FINE-TUNE THE LEVELNESS

Pool tables tend to settle and over time can become off level. If this happens it is a simple matter to re-level it. Using a pool cue, slowly cue a ball from one side to the other along both ends of the table; do not use english (see **A Rookie's Guide to Playing Winning Pool** on how english affects the ball). Using a cue is important, instead of hand rolling the ball, to prevent unwanted ball spin. Watch to see if the ball rolls toward one end or the other. The ball will, of course, roll toward the low end if one exists. Shim beneath the leg or legs (see pages 21-23) of the low end until the ball rolls true. Careful, though, it should not take much adjustment.

Now cue a ball from one end to the other along both sides of the table. Shim beneath the leg of the low side until the ball rolls true in that direction. Very little roll-off should be detected other than a small amount of cloth (nap) roll as the ball slows to a stop. BCA regulations allow for one ball diameter roll-off for the length of the table. Any table can easily be leveled to beat that tolerance.

Rails, aprons, pockets, and slate screws are not designed to support the weight of the entire table, so a table should never be lifted from any part except the cabinet or frame. Any short automobile jack will work, and jack only at the center of a side or end of the table (Figure 5-71).

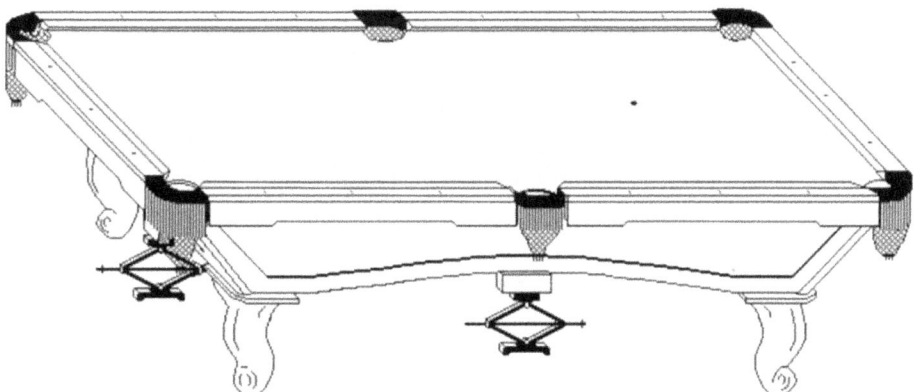

Figure 5-71 *Table jacking points.*

BOOKS by Mose Duane

A Rookie's Guide to
    Pool Table Maintenance and Repair
    Buying or Selling a Pool Table
    Pool Table Assembly
    Playing Winning Pool

Novels
    JC's Last Chance
    Coyote Stands
    Something Substantial
    The Great Pool Table Heist of Arizona
        (Obama and the Dixie Chicks)
   Bigg Dick: Real Justise
   Pussy Willows: A Bigg Dick Novel

Available
    phx**billiards**.com
    amazon.com and Kindle
    barnes**and**noble.com and Nook
    Google Books
    Apple Books
    Kobo
    Etcetera

ABOUT THE AUTHOR

Mose Duane was awarded Writer's Digest National Self-Published Book Awards' certificate of merit for The Billiard Guidebook (Pool Table Maintenance and Repair).

He has written four *A Rookie's Guide to* billiard books and six novels. He lives in Arizona with his lovely wife Karen.

www.ingramcontent.com/pod-product-compliance
Lightning Source LLC
Chambersburg PA
CBHW081501040426
42446CB00016B/3340